# FENCES

## HARRY SYMONS

Author of
*Three Ships West, The Bored Meeting, etc.*

Illustrations by
C. W. JEFFERYS, R.C.A., LL.D.

## THE RYERSON PRESS - TORONTO

PRINTED AND BOUND IN CANADA
BY THE RYERSON PRESS, TORONTO

# GENERAL INTRODUCTION

THE MATERIAL NECESSARY to this work was organized, assembled and, in the main, originated through the efforts of my father-in-law, the late William Perkins Bull, K.C., B.A., LL.D., in collaboration with one of our most famous Canadian artists, the late Charles W. Jefferys, R.C.A., O.S.A., LL.D. The former, before his death, had already become internationally renowned through the writing and publication of his historical series concerning Peel County, Ontario, a series which it is doubtful has ever been equalled in detail and magnitude for a work of that kind.

Dr. Perkins Bull, being the initiator of the project, invited Dr. Jefferys to join him in the undertaking, and it was typical of both that they fully realized its potentiality and scope. It is interesting to note that the study embraces and includes, in considerable measure, the last great effort, not only combined, but individually, of these two distinguished Canadians.

Assisting them in their research were two other well-known citizens, in the persons of the Director of the Dominion Experimental Farms at Ottawa, Edgar S. Archibald, B.A., B.S.A., LL.D., D.Sc., F.R.S.C., and Eric Ross Arthur, M.A., B.Arch. (Liverpool), F.R.I.B.A., Professor of Architectural Design at the University of Toronto. It is a pleasure to acknowledge herewith the toil undertaken by them, and to thank them for their very considerable contributions.

Oddly enough, at first blush no subject would appear

to hold less possibility or attraction than the subject of fences. Yet the more one thinks about it, and the more one explores, the more fascinating it becomes. This magnificent group of drawings represents the last great collective work of Dr. Jefferys, a fact that somehow adds an aura of value and timelessness that may appeal in a sentimental way to many of us.

The story of fences goes back through the dim ages to the very beginning of man. Always there have been fences, or dividing walls, or stockades, or bulwarks, or hedges, or contrivances of one separating kind or another. The Great Wall of China; Hadrian's wall in northern England, built from coast to coast, to keep out the marauders from the north; Indian stockades; and on and on through history from earliest Biblical times, through stone fences, dry walls that move with the frozen land, brick fences, wooden fences, wire fences, stump, hedge, concrete, turf, and even to privet, box, locust, cactus, fuchsia, laurel and hawthorn, and finally, to our single strand, ridiculous-looking but economical and efficient electric fence of today. What a story they have to tell. What changes they have seen.

Dr. Jefferys remarked that it had always been a dream of his to produce and illustrate a book on fences, and that, from time to time on his trips, he spent hours drawing fences instead of painting in colour. He pointed out that amongst the few municipal officers which the government of Upper Canada permitted were the fence viewers. Two were usually deputed to inspect the fences of each township or section thereof. He felt that he and Dr. Perkins Bull were like the old time fence viewers, because, in not always agreeing, they must surely be in the line of tradition.

The Old Testament abounds in vignettes of walled gardens and running water. But from Cyrus to Peter the

Great actual descriptions of fences and walls were sadly sparing, although it is known that stone walls were built not for privacy but for protection, and that, as in China today, there were many fences of saplings, laths, long sharp stakes or even palisades.

The word fence derives from the Latin *fendere,* to ward off, implying a confining or enclosing against human or animal intrusion.

"Zion is a fortress encircled by walls and bastions," as the Israelites so aptly said. The Mosaic law threatened with a curse him who removed his neighbour's landmark, or fence.

In France, at the Chateau of Villandry, in Touraine, three gardens have been built and preserved and become famous, each typical of its time. The herb garden of the Middle Ages, with its mint, borage, and thyme, its sage, marjoram, and rosemary, its rue, camomile, rhubarb, hives, and murmuring bees. It is surrounded by a tunnelled hedge. Then came the garden of the Renaissance, with box hedges, yews and mazes, fountains and terraces. Around it is a stone wall, with a border of clipped trees. And, lastly, we have the modern kitchen garden gay with flowers, and a low coping about it. All three gardens are protected by moats.

The ancient Britons and Gauls were skilled in the use of wattles and mud walls, but it was from the Romans they learned of hedging and ditching, stone work and brick work.

The author of *Estate Fences* chose as a fitting motto "Ever Fence the Right." He went on to say that in Roman times meadows and pasture lands, as Virgil suggests, were not enclosed. Livestock, attended by herdsmen, was pastured in the open spaces. Wide stretches of the Roman Campagna, unfenced and unbounded, attest the same fact. Even in Britain, where wild beasts infested the forests, sheep and cattle were folded only at night, and only gardens were fenced from animal marauders.

Sir Thomas More, in his *Utopia,* reflects sadly in Henry VIII's time upon the increase of pasture,

> by which your sheep, which are naturally mild and kept in order, may be said now to devour man and unpeople not only villages but towns; for whenever it is found of any soil yield a softer and richer wool than the ordinary, there the nobility and gentry, and even these holy men the abbots, not contented with the old rents which their farms yielded, nor thinking it enough that they, living at their ease, do no good to the public, resolved to do it hurt instead of good. They stop the course of agriculture, destroying houses and towns, reserving only the churches, and enclose grounds that they may lodge their sheep in them.

Robert Frost wrote that truly memorable thought "Good fences make good neighbours," whilst George Herbert said "Love your neighbour, yet pull not down your hedge." No wiser words were ever spoken.

In Canada rural fences have grown up with the country, whilst materials used and construction methods varied. But it is singularly correct that a farmer may well be known by his fences. A glance at road fences will usually reveal the sort of farmer who tills beyond them. Upstanding, well maintained fences indicate progressive yeomen, well cultivated fields and contented live stock, whereas neglected fences go with tumble down barns, undernourished cattle, weedy fields, poverty and general inefficiency. A well built fence promotes cordiality amongst neighbours and is insurance against friction. Poor fences do, indeed, make bad neighbours.

Some fences are almost indigenous to the localities wherein they are located. In Ontario such would seem to be the case with stump, snake and straight rail fences. They seem to blend into and be a part of the landscape itself. They are efficient in a careless, improvised way. Their aesthetic effect is great, for they are obviously home-made. They tell of trees felled, stumps uprooted, stones removed, rails split and new ground broken and made ready for seeding.

The earliest local fence was the red man's palisade, as also it was the primitive fence of China, of Africa and, indeed, of Europe too. It fitted into but did not dominate nature, just as the coureurs-de-bois fitted into the Indian life of Canada. In 1660 a palisade protected Dollard and his sixteen gallant companions in their heroic stand.

Father Gabriel Sagard, a contemporary of Champlain, gives details in his *Journey to Huronia* which suggest that palisades and Indian type fencing were developed long before the advent of the white man. He goes on to say:

In this stretch of country there are about twenty-five towns and villages. Some of these are not enclosed or shut in, while others are fortified by strong wooden palisades in three rows, interlaced into one another and reinforced within by large, thick pieces of bark to a height of eight or nine feet, and at the bottom there are great trunks of trees placed lengthwise resting on strong, short forks made from tree trunks . . . and defend their ramparts with great courage and skill.

As will already be seen the fence is inseparable from the history of men. One might even trace it back to the lower animals, for what is a beaver dam but a water fence?

Fences have always been inextricably interwoven with our Canadian military history. One of the earliest hostile encounters was Champlain's fight with the Iroquois on the western shore of Lake Champlain, in the year 1600. The Indians prepared for battle by building their palisade, from behind which they poured a deadly flight of arrows upon the invaders.

At Ticonderoga, in 1758, the British regiments flung themselves in vain against the breastwork of logs (a snake-fence) built by Montcalm around his camp. In Pontiac's war it was from the shelter of palisades that Gladwin and his scanty garrison successfully defended Detroit throughout the longest siege of any fortified post in our history. In old Quebec barricades across the narrow streets of the lower town held back the American Revolutionists under Arnold and Montgomery in their assault, on New Year's Eve in 1775. And throughout the War of 1812 the fence, in various forms, proved an important factor in deciding the issue of many a combat. The forts along the Niagara frontier were mainly earthworks surrounded by deep ditches, and, sometimes, as at Fort Erie, reinforced by masonry, on the slopes of which palisades were planted. The reconstruction of Fort York at Toronto, Fort Wellington at Prescott, and Forts George and Erie show clearly how they looked.

In 1813 the victory at Chateauguay was due in great part to the abatis of felled trees and the log breastworks behind which de Salaberry and "Red George" Macdonell, with less than 500 Voltigeurs and *Fenc*ibles withstood and routed the attack of some 7,000 Americans.

In the bloody battle of Lundy's Lane a rail fence was largely responsible for the defeat of the British. In a letter written a few days after the battle the Colonel gives due credit to the fence. His letter reads:

It was then evening, but moonlight. General Brown turned to me and said, "Colonel Miller, take your regiment and storm that work, and take it." His answer, "I'll try, Sir," became famous in American history. "I had short of 300 men . . . I, however, immediately obeyed the order. We could see their slow matches and port-fires burning and ready . . . we advanced upon the mouths of their cannon. It happened that there was an old rail fence on the site where we approached, undiscovered by the enemy, with a small growth of shrubbery by the fence, and within less than two rod of

[ x ]

the cannon. I then very cautiously ordered my men to rest across the fence, take good aim, fire, and rush, which was done in good style. Not one man at the cannons was left to put fire to them.

Thus, ironically, with the help of the Canadian rail fence and its shrubbery of raspberry bushes, golden rod and aster, were our defenders driven from their position.

Had you been a British regular at St. Denis, in 1837, you certainly would have cursed in true army fashion the fence that sheltered the "Patriotes" in their successful resistance to the attack of the Government Forces. Fences also figured in the advance of the Canadians Militia at Ridgeway, and at the breastworks of the Fenian invaders along the ridge.

At Batoche, the site of the last armed conflict on Canadian soil, one could trace, a few years ago, along the coulées, the rifle pits and mouldering logs where the Métis rebels of 1885 crouched and for three days held off the attacking troops.

From then onward in our history to date fences and stockades were no longer needed to restrain attack. The blood curdling war-whoop of the Indian, and his dreadful feats of scalping, were things of a bygone era.

## The Evolution of Canadian Fences

Deer pounds and buffalo pounds were a form of fencing originated and used by the Indians long before the advent of the white man to North America. They were, in effect, a form of trap into which the unsuspecting animals were driven until they reached a bottle neck, where they were quickly brought down with bow and arrow. Their construction was ingenious and haphazard, but successful for their purpose. The great Cree chieftain, Poundmaker, so famous in our history of the far West, was so named because of his craftsmanship in the making of buffalo pounds. His thus being named indicates the importance the Indian mind attached to this early type of fencing for the securing of food.

Abraham Lincoln in his day was affectionately known as "the rail splitter," because of his prowess at this very tricky job. Even in those times, snake rail fences meandered up hill and down dale. They turned awkward corners adroitly, dodging boulders and huge trees. Because of their sharp angles and interlocking joints they were strong and solid. But they had two drawbacks; they sheltered weeds in their corners; they took up a lot of room. But against this, in harvest time they served the harvesters wonderfully well as eating and resting places in the hot weather.

Straight rail fences were, of course, an adaptation of the snake fence and were built in much the same way, but lacked the two bad features of the latter. They succeeded the snake fence which, in its turn, succeeded the stump fence, which comprised simply large tree stumps piled in a row, thus forming a type of obstacle very difficult for livestock to break through. But probably the earliest pioneer fence of all was known as the brush fence. The construction simply consisted of piling brush, logs and roots around the settler's clearing. They were the easiest and the cheapest of all, in actual labour, but the cattle went through them, and the pigs went under them, unless they were according to Squire McLaughlin's specifications. Presiding in a Caledon township police court, the Squire ruled that a brush fence to be legal "must be forty feet wide, and damned high."

Stumping bees were organized in the long ago pioneer days, at which the neighbours assembled, including their families, and their teams of oxen, and over-sized bulging hampers of food, consisting of cooked hams and chickens, home-made pork sausages, doughnuts fried in lard, pies, cakes, buttermilk and raspberry vinegar. The latter was known as shrub, a name for it brought from the old country. Mostly the oxen were called Buck and Bright, the former worked on the off side and Bright on the nigh. Some ox yokes were fitted on the neck and shoulders, whilst other teams took the strain on their heads and horns. The soil would be loosened about the stumps and all except the tap roots cut. Then in went the teams of oxen, and, with a good "all together" steady pull, out came another useful section of fencing. After a tremendous supper the local fiddler cleared a space and "called off" for the dancing that usually followed, accompanied by lusty singing and genuine olden time frolic.

The snake rail fence, too, was abandoned in favour of the straight rail because the boundary lines between farms, carelessly placed in pioneer days, were even more strictly defined as time went on.

Settlers soon enough learned to peel the bark off the fencing material, since, freed of bark and the moisture it held, the wood lasted much longer. The lower transverse sleepers, and rails too, were often anchored with boulders and thus kept from contact with the damp ground.

Then there was the bull-nay fence, which was so called because it was said it could withstand the onrush of a bull. In construction it was much like the straight rail fence, as will be seen from Dr. Jefferys' drawing.

Still another type was made of sixty foot logs, with ends overlapping at different intervals. It demanded, as one might well imagine, skill in construction, plus a plentiful supply of good, straight, evenly-girthed logs, but it formed a simple and effective barrier.

Barbed wire, first patented in 1873, in its original form was indeed a different commodity than that of today. It was made from flat strips of metal, notched on alternate edges about every six inches. A far cry from the barbed wire of varying weights of our time! To begin with, livestock suffered severely before they gradually became accustomed through generations to respect its possibility to seriously injure. And the same applied to the present-day electric fence. Its appearance is so innocently misleading, but its effect can be devastating. In the same slow way the cattle learned to shun it, to a point that quite often now the fact of the single strand of wire being strung up on posts with white insulating bobbins is quite sufficient to keep the animals away, regardless of the wire not being electrified.

Gradually the era of the wooden fence in its many forms is passing. The demise, however, is usually a cheery one, for on a winter's evening what is more delightful for a comforting fire than pine knots or oak stump roots or cedar rails blazing away right merrily in a large open fireplace, bringing warmth and contentment to the farmer's family circle.

As for barbed wire, it is the post that gives the greatest concern. Generally speaking, wooden posts are short lived and rot off at ground level, whilst iron posts are costly. As for steel, hard steel is given to corrosion, whilst soft steel bends. Concrete makes a highly satisfactory anchorage, whereas dry or mortared stone is handsome and durable, although costly.

In cities, towns and villages the board fence was popular in its day. Among the well to do it was, and still is, much used for paddocks, pastures and along the roadside. Even when weatherbeaten, grey and lichen-grown it is pleasing to the eye, and will last for decades if well built. In days gone by they were revenue producing investments, used for advertising in bright paint such then popular medicines as Radway's Ready Relief, Empire Horse and Cattle Food, Burdock Blood Bitters, to name a few.

One of the most enduring and beautiful of walls is that made of stones or boulders, without mortar, known as the dry stone wall, as opposed to the mortared wall. The former could be made from the stones ploughed up in the adjoining fields, and they required no foundation, as the land upon which they were built moved. Moisture had no effect upon them, nor frost, nor ice, whilst the mortared stone, concrete, or stucco wall needed to be carried upon a solid foundation, in depth well below average frost line. The cost of the latter ran far beyond the pocket of the average farmer, as well as the same type of wall surmounted with iron work, or that made of cast iron throughout. In the main these are confined to country estates, larger city homes, the enclosing of ornamental lawns, public buildings, parks and gardens. Handsome examples of such are the walls surrounding St. James' Cathedral, old Trinity College, and Osgoode Hall, all in Toronto, and to name but a very few. Proposals to move the famous and attractive Osgoode Hall landmark met with such violent opposition that it was rapidly dropped. The tradition of formidable fences surrounding court houses and public buildings is an old British one.

The wooden picket fence so dear to New England, and once so popular in Ontario, still finds favour in Quebec. One of Toronto's finest picket fences surrounded the property of old Mr. Barlow Cumberland on Front Street. Another fine fence, although the building it encompassed has long since disappeared, still stands on Front Street, around the Canadian Pacific Express Offices, the old site of our Government House. It is of iron hoops bent parallel, their ends set in the ground, and supported by wooden posts.

The removal of residential fences would appear to be an idea of Americans to open up finer vistas of lawns and gardens, and to turn a whole neighbourhood into a sort of park. However this result cannot be achieved, obviously, without a loss of privacy, coupled with the fact that one or two owners amongst a group, may become indifferent to the appearance of their property and so spoil the overall effect.

[ xv ]

"A hedge between keeps friendship green," sang the poet. While there are many fine hedges in Ontario, Canadians as a whole do not seem to take to them enthusiastically Comparatively few plant hedges around their dwellings. In former days Ontario had its quota, notably in the Oakville area and around the shores of Lake Simcoe.

Experienced and skilful "hedgers and ditchers" abound in Europe, but not in North America. The introduction of hedges to North America is thought by some to trace back to George Washington. But the commonest in Ontario grew from seeds windblown along the old rail fences.

Cedar makes a clean evergreen hedge that demands little trimming, and, being indigenous, is very hardy. Box and barberry are also seen, as well as hawthorn. In 1824 Daniel Johnson brought from Ireland, tied in his red bandana, a handful of hawthorn berries. He planted them along the northwest forty rod on the farm in Chinguacousy Township, in the County of Peel. The resultant hedge grew and flourished, and has been for well over a century its only road fence there. It grew and became a landmark, and gave its name of Hawthorne Lodge to the homestead of Bartholomew Hill Bull, in whose family the property still remains.

The locust hedge, seen here and there, is indeed a pleasant feature of our landscape. It is almost impenetrable, and its exquisite white, scented blossoms and delicate, ferny foliage are a delight to the beholder.

Quetton St. George, a French emigré, who fled his country during the Revolution, settled north of the town of York. He imported rare hedge shrubs from Europe for his estate near Wilcox Lake, where a considerable section of hedge, eight or ten feet high, still lines the roadside.

As has already been said, there are many kinds of hedges

used not only for purposes of privacy but for fencing as well. One finds them in many lands throughout the world. Some of them are ugly, but serviceable, whilst others have a rare beauty in leaf and in flower.

## THE HUMOROUS SIDE

As a rule there is nothing especially subtle about line-fence humour. In *Le Rire,* of Paris, Henri Bergeon discusses the comic element which exists in mere mechanical arrangements of things or events. Man is a "mechanical" animal.

That there may be something comical in the idea of a barrier fence, or boundary dividing things which should not be divided, was quite clearly illustrated in the case of the Indian tribes of the Middle West against that strong, invisible fence, the International Boundary Line. As soon as the public realized the situation, the Indian claim evoked a laugh, not of ridicule but of sympathy. Why should any fence or boundary be required to separate the tribes who, for a millennium, had roamed freely up and down the great continent of America, undeterred by artificial barriers, or even by invisible parallels of latitude? Examined for even a brief moment through Indian eyes, the Boundary, the Forty-Ninth Parallel, and all or any adjuncts thereto became ridiculous.

Of course the attitude of livestock and wild animals toward fences cannot be said to be a humorous one. To the occasional bystander it can, however, sometimes seem amusing, but more often it is prone to be annoying. The farm animal naturally regards any type of wall or barrier as simply something to somehow bypass, or to crawl under, or climb, or jump over. Cows unhesitatingly use their horns to remove rail fence riders, but toward the fence as such they rarely seem to have animosity or mischievous intent. They merely wish, if you please, to graze in that next succulent field of whatever it may be, which is so much more desirable than the scrubby, grazed-over field they are presently in. But in human beings it is quite a different story. There is some imp, some age-old urge, call it what you will, that actively dislikes fences. "Is it elves?" asks Robert Frost. Perhaps he may be right, for some strange spirit of mischief is ever and always eager to pull them down, not only on Hallowe'en, but on election nights as well. And almost the first thing the mob does in a time of public disturbance is to tear away whatever serves as a barrier against them. Perhaps it is the primeval urge for freedom from all restraint that smoulders but never quite dies in the hearts of all of us.

When you come to think of it the invisible, but none the less real, customs barriers set up by governments, are in reality nothing but fences of a kind. And, to the poor citizen, extremely annoying fences, too. The customs office may almost be considered a "stile," or "gateway" in the customs wall. Occasionally impatient folk refuse to wait their turn to go through all the tedious and aggravating rigamarole set up by officialdom (which often is a form of bottle-neck), and organize to hurdle the customs wall surreptitiously. Perhaps they cross at some unofficial border point where no one sees them. Possibly slyly and covertly under the robe of darkness. Or perchance they don't declare all their taxable possessions or purchases. No doubt there is some personal hazard and betimes ultimate cost, too. But its like a game or a gamble, seemingly, to many. The excitement of it appears to lure people "just for the fun of the thing," many of whom delight in an odd type of adventure where financially they need not give the added duty charge even a second thought. Sometimes we have heard of ladies of high station and much wealth who have vied with one another to see who could get through unnoticed with the most swag. Surely this minor mischief is the stirring of that same imp, that fence breaker already bespoken?

Steeplechasing is not exactly a form of humour, but it certainly is a pleasure, and good fun. The "lepper" from the Curragh, or the stony fields of West Cork, seems to take an almost positive delight in spurning stone walls as though they were bad jokes.

Some animals, of course, make fences look funny. Such was the case of an old billy goat belonging to Dr. Jim McKay of Elmbank, in Peel County, in the days of long ago. Strangely enough, this strange old goat possessed an ever-recurrent thirst for hard liquor, of all things, coupled with an uncanny ability to climb a snake fence and walk along the top rail. In the afternoons old "Billy" would leave the McKay farm house and trot happily along his unique, self-selected highway a matter of a mile, or thereabouts, to Button's Tavern at the Claireville five corners. The tavern was a large, white, two-storied, frame building made popular by its many local patrons. Generally there was a scramble as to who would stand the first treat— and old Billy was always included, and never missed a drink if he could help it. After a goodly number of rounds old Billy, not quite as sure-footed as on arrival, would think of home. He was invariably the first to leave. Of course the assembled guests were always intrigued by the prospects of old Billy's homeward journey. No matter how wobbly he was he always refused any highway except the top of the rail fence. Needless to say, it quite often took him several attempts before he could even successfully mount his self-appointed pathway. His frantic efforts to stay on top were even more ridiculous. Finally he would make off, slowly and cautiously, with much staggering hesitation and wild swayings from side to side, and lustily cheered by his convivial hosts. A slight unpremeditated slip often sent him collapsing to the ground in a heap; but after a maudlin interval he would again with difficulty mount his beloved fence and thus continue his journey the whole way home. It was, apparently, a comic, unforgettable blending of incongruity, coupled with haughty dignity.

Admittedly the pig is, to put it mildly, a reluctant swimmer. But much as it dislikes water, it seemingly dislikes fences even more. In Peel County there was, so the story goes, a lanky brood sow that, rather than be stopped by a mere fence, used to swim around the end of one which extended its last two rails into a river. The current was strong, but so was this pesky pig's determination to spend an hour in the inviting potato patch on the other side.

Removing gates and throwing down bars were, and still are favourite Hallowe'en pranks. Even old-time buggies and sundry farm equipment have been known to find their way to the top of barn and house roofs, so that the owners on going out the following morning were flabbergasted to see such items perched precariously but complete on top of the ridge. The art of the thing was, apparently, to dissemble the article into as many pieces as possible, and then, having transferred them individually, to reassemble them in their new location. One must admit to suddenly come upon an old buggy perched atop one's house or barn roof must have been amazing in its effect, to say the least.

In a sense the moving of gates or tearing down of barriers were and are, not so much humorous as malicious. True, little damage ensued, perhaps, but the collecting of straying livestock left much to be desired. An unpopular man just never did rightly know on whose land he would find his cattle. Maybe they were on an adjoining farm, or, perhaps, miles away. Or it might be that someone else's animals were quietly eating their heads off in his favourite corn patch.

The following clipping appeared in the *Colonial Advocate* of July 11, 1827:

It is really surprising what pleasure some people find in giving their neighbours trouble. The advertisement of William Robertson of this day is intended as a public warning to one of his neighbours, before applying for a warrant, who has thrown down his fences, made a foot and horse path of his enclosed fields, and disregarded his complaints against such unmerited and illegal trespasses.

Times haven't greatly changed in such matters, nor people for the matter of that, since the foregoing sentiment was expressed. There will always be, as there always has been, the nigger in the woodpile, so to speak; the misfits in the community who make life more difficult for those around them. This must always have applied, from Peru to China, from Labrador to darkest Africa, and doubtless never will change until the inhabitants of the world are obliterated finally—doubtless through the last mad gesture of the last and worst misfit of them all. One might almost feel safe in guessing what nationality he might be.

## THE LEGAL ASPECTS

Neighbours' quarrels, like international wars, often grow from boundary disputes. It is true that surveyors cut concession lines along road allowances in which they placed corner posts to clearly mark each lot, but they certainly did not survey or stake out the other boundary lines of the various farms. When a settler wanted to build his line fence it can be readily seen what a ticklish job it could be, unless his neighbours were on hand and were agreed.

Pioneer holdings were often large, and frequently only partially cleared. A few feet one way or another on a bushland farm, like a shilling on a horse race, made very

[ xxi ]

little difference. But as Canada developed, and this, we presume, applied to all countries, line fences, barriers and boundaries of all kinds assumed greater importance. The early confusion in this country was perpetuated further by snake fences. A United States farmer estimated six acres as the loss, or "fence waste" on twenty acres of land. As the owners became more appreciative of the producing possibilities, and, hence, the cash value of their land, the importance of the exact boundary line was increased.

But it seems true that unhealthy quarrels were just as frequent over straying stock as over disputed boundaries. Pound law gave the farmer the right to claim any stock he found straying upon his land. (The possibilities were, shall we say, endless and unlimited.)

No wonder, therefore, that the "fence question" really came into its own. What questions! What headaches! What problems! The sturdy pioneers asked what stock should roam at large, if any, and whether a man should fence his own stock "in" or that of his neighbours "out"? If someone had no stock at all to keep in, need he build a fence at all? If the neighbours kept ill-mannered, breachy stock (and there were and are many such—and meaning beasts that seem to spend their lives intent upon escaping through or breaching their enclosing barriers) should not such neighbour keep it under control? Should it not be his responsibility completely? And if wild stock broke down a road or line fence, who then should repair the said fence? Obviously the stock wouldn't. It simply went dreamily on looking for more ways to get to wherever it wasn't. And the whole thing just pyramided, and snowballed onward and ever upward with the increase of settlers, the increase of crops, and the consequent increase of livestock. Fights, lawsuits, spite and thoroughly bad blood generally prevailed.

Have you ever sat quietly and watched a herd of cattle, today, in this era, grazing close at hand? This is digressing for a moment, but in a sense it does one good to digress. If you will be patient and wait long enough you will almost certainly note one of the herd which is that undesirable of undesirables, the breacher type. Often she will have an oddity about her, such as one horn up and one horn down. She has, when you get to know her, a sort of slinky look about her. A kind of defiance, if you will. Perhaps life, and the herd have not been kindly to her. Who knows? But she inevitably seems restless and discontented. So often she wanders off by herself and noses along the fence lines. If she can reach over she reaches over. If things give a little, she persuades them to give more. If she can poke her head through a strand wire fence she will certainly do so, and certainly do her best to enlarge the opening. If it's an electric fence you somehow feel she almost lures the younger and more innocent of the herd over in the hope, by mistake, they will touch the live wire. If they do, and it *is* live, and they jump, all well and good, she stays away from it. But if they *don't* jump, she seems to know the whole fence is a farce, and proceeds to wade through it without let or hindrance, like a dowager duchess under full sail. And with a smug look about her, too. She epitomizes the breacher, the malcontent, and is diametrically the opposite to the well fed, well tended, sleek and well contented herds whose productivity is so much greater and who, to help them toward contentment, have gentle music piped to them as they stand in their immaculate barn stalls, placidly chewing their cuds in supreme bliss what time they are being joyfully milked mechanically.

But back to the fights, the lawsuits, the bad blood and the endless spite. Things had reached, finally, such an unhappy pass that in 1834 an act of William IV provided for the appointment of "fit and discreet persons" as the "fence viewers" already mentioned, to determine what should be a lawful fence. They were given extraordinary powers, and could order the extent of fence to be built, or repaired by either or both of the aroused contesting parties. And their decision as to the quality and type of fence, its precise location, and the time it must be finished was definite and final.

And the "fence viewers" had similar jurisdiction as to drains. They could administer oaths, examine and cross-examine witnesses under oath, collect fines, award damages, and determine costs. By the year 1882 the recital of their many duties filled several pages of the Revised Statutes of Ontario. But for all their heavy and long labours, and considering the weight of their authority, it is amazing to learn that, under the Act, they received only two dollars each for a day's work. And no suggestion of an expense account either. Even the name of this "near-magisterial" office is practically forgotten, whereas in the not-far-distant yesterdays "fence viewers" were men of weight, importance and prestige.

Feuds between neighbours, because of line fences, or broken down barriers, often lasted for years. Sometimes they were transmitted from generation to generation and, if complicated by political or religious differences, at times led to violence and bloodshed. The various types of farming that neighbours practised, their industry or their shiftlessness, their balance of fairness and meanness, their sheer poverty or relative prosperity, all contributed occasions for quarrelling. If people were already hostile, the line fence was an ever and always available open sore. Of course it would have been simple to call a surveyor, or "fence viewer." But this would have cost money, and the pioneers were pretty thrifty, even tight fisted, although generous. Their fences were rarely if ever erected following a survey, and seldom satisfied anyone but the actual builder. The costs of upkeep and apportionment thereof, as well as the type of barrier, invited contrary opinions. When crops and pastures lay side by side, the owner of the cattle was much less interested in strong fencing than the owner of the growing crop. And there were so often those breachy-type cattle already bespoken. And a wood lot next to a field of grain offered a similar problem.

The fence viewers formed a board. Any two of them could make a formal and binding award. They could dictate by whom or where the fence was to be built, of exactly what materials, of what type, as well as to height and strength. And they could even set the exact time limit for the construction and for its repair. But there was one mixed blessing excluded, they had no executive power. They could, in the last analysis, merely hand down a decision and then the matter was out of their hands.

To begin with their decision led to endless turmoil because the law provided that one might erect a line fence and then bill his neighbour for half the costs. As one can imagine, such procedure had endless possibilities. Generally, of course, it was quite impossible to get anywhere without going to law. Or a person might find it cheaper to pay the statutory charge than to build the fence himself, especially when materials rose in price and it became unlikely that he could collect from his neighbour. Finally, in 1855, the fixing of the cost was left to the discretion of the admirable fence viewers.

Needless to relate, squabbles and bickering over cattle as has been said, were endless. A poor barrier was merely an open invitation to livestock to breach it, and where that one infuriating breaching cow-boss led, the rest of the herd followed with happy docility. Breachy horses were forever jumping over into the next fellow's oats or hay. In fact they still do. And nearly every farm had that solid nuisance of a breachy cow, or steer, with a board hanging over its eyes so that it could not get a square look at a fence to jump over it or push it down. It wasn't at all unusual to see a horse handicapped by a poke between its front legs, or with its head tied down, or a chain fastened to one of its front fetlocks, or with the two feet on one or other side tethered together with ropes so that it could neither rear nor gallop. But the casual and indifferent neighbour didn't bother about such niceties. If his animals could find it convenient to graze on old Zeb's property, so much the better. Old Zeb was downright mean, anyway, and probably deserved it. But that wasn't what old Zeb thought, and of course he was doubtless more often right than wrong. The possibilities in the thing were, and still are, just endless.

Impounding of cattle, damage to crops, and consequent ill-feeling led to innumerable lawsuits amongst cantankerous neighbours. Usually the damages were small in most cases, and all the litigant got out of it was the satisfaction (?) of putting his next door neighbour to trouble and expense.

"Trespass roads" and "rights of way" also often caused friction. Old time trails, doubtless originated by the Indians, followed no survey. They generally made a bee-line to their objectives. In fact many of our Ontario highways of today still follow Indian or pioneer trails of the long ago, quite regardless of surveys made after they had become main travelled roads.

But the trouble was that "trespass roads" and trails unhappily always sought dry land, and avoided such things as steep and stony places, as well as swamps, creek beds and broken country. For instance, Yonge Street, the main thoroughfare in Toronto, leading from Lake Ontario, at Toronto Bay, clear through to Lake Simcoe lying about sixty miles northerly, Yonge Street sought to avoid Hogg's Hollow and the Holland Marsh. The former being a deep, river valley at the north of Toronto, and the latter being low-lying boggy land on the southern shores of Lake Simcoe. But good dry level land is, needless to say, what the agriculturist prefers to cultivate. So when Zeb and old Will, in the long gone days, took to fencing their fields, the trespass roads and trails were driven down into the swamps and up onto the hills. This merely served as fuel for further irritation and local resentment. When a settler found himself cut off from the dry trail he was accustomed to follow, and was forced to haul his cordwood and his crops to market through bogs and over hills, or when his cattle's short cut to their drinking place was suddenly barred, it is no wonder that a sense of grievance and injustice might impel him to cut the offending fence. In many ways who could blame him?

In dealing with Ontario fences one must remember that in the early days the physical contour of some of that province's counties made settlement extraordinarily difficult because of the lack of any travel and transportation facilities. The local countryside all too frequently was a dismal succession of steep hills, and deep heavily wooded ravines, chock full of stumps, mudholes, boulders, stones and uninviting stretches of muskeg. In well-settled localities the grading of hills, filling of holes, bridging of muskeg and removal of stones and stumps was pretty well accomplished late in the nineteenth century. Meantime, travel was rendered extremely difficult by the farmers who, quite naturally, insisted on fencing every arable acre, thus cutting off many useful old trails and short cuts. It would have been nothing short of a miracle had there been no fence cutting, no black eyes, no disgruntled neighbours, and no lawsuits.

As might well be expected the average pioneer, settler, or even farmer of today, was and still is, ignorant when it comes to law. Many were blissfully unaware of the fact that though a fence may constitute a boundary line it is not, in point of fact, a legal boundary. If, then, an old-established line fence happened to enclose an acre or so of the next fellow's farm, the owner feared he had lost it forever. This, of course, was not the case. Later surveys showed just how inaccurately placed were the old line fences. Original survey lines were sometimes cut on trees, and of course these in due course died and were cut down. Even the surveyors' stakes became completely overgrown or otherwise disappeared. And although it is true that a row of trees, or a fence, gave a rough and ready idea of the boundary, it could indeed not be relied upon for accuracy. Nor were shallow streams legal barriers. Creeks shifted their channels. Spring freshets and heavy rains wore away the banks on one side, depositing soil and gravel upon the other. When road making began in earnest, it was found that many fences encroached not only on neighbouring farms but upon the road allowances as well, and the early records are full of cases of road obstruction. Of course, the pioneers and settlers figured they had squatters' rights covering any land they had occupied for a long time. It was no easy job to convince old Will or Jabez that "time does not run against the sovereign." In other words, by undisputed possession of another man's land for a number of years, say ten or twenty, or whatever the law of the particular district stipulated, one might acquire title to land previously belonging to another person, but definitely not so if it were land belonging to the Crown.

Sometimes a road allowance was too narrow and the authorities would acquire land from the neighbouring farmer. Again, sometimes a generous owner would temporarily allow the public to use part of his land for a highway, and then, afraid that he would lose it altogether, or following some squabble not in any way relative to the fence itself, would decide to fence it in again.

However, there was one matter at least on which town councils had to deliberate, to wit, what constituted a legal fence. Of course the ideal fence, "horse-high, bull-strong, and skunk-tight," was not too easy to agree on, or in fact, to erect. Bush fences were never legal, but log fences appear to have given satisfaction.

Early legislation goes into minute detail, and deals entirely with rail fences. The bottom rail was to be within four inches of the ground and the rails not more than four inches apart, and the whole fence had to be staked and ridered.

In those times cattle were kept "handy by" for protection against wolves and bears. On the other hand, droves of half wild hogs were allowed to roam at large in the woods. Each hog was a match and more than a match for two or three wolves, and few fences were strong enough to keep the hogs in. In fact they became such a nuisance that municipal councils passed by-laws to keep them under restraint. They had become accustomed to roam the village streets, and in York itself gardens not enclosed by tight fences were often ruined by them. First the larger towns, then soon the villages, banned them, and finally they were shut out altogether.

The English periodical *Country Life* in its November 8th issue, 1956, in an article by W. J. Weston, discusses the laws in England regarding stiles. He commences with the old English verse:

Jog on, jog on the foot-path way,
And merrily hent the stile-a:
A merry heart goes all the day,
Your sad tires in a mile-a.

Then he goes on to answer a correspondent's question as to whether he may repair or alter a stile to make it more convenient, as he is old and finds difficulty in going over it as it is. The answer appears to be that indeed he may. Apparently it was written long ago, by Chief Justice Coke, that "Reason is the life of the law; nay, the common law itself is nothing but reason." In England, a right-of-way apparently connotes the right to pass over the lands of another, by kissing gate, by stile or by posts crossing the barriers, and these should not be less convenient than possible or than have existed in the past. A 13th century report is, "If A. places a fence where his neighbour B. hath a driftway to his common of pasture, then B. commits no tort if, freshly on the placing thereof, he do abate it in the daytime." This, as far as this goes, seems to clear up the whole thing neatly, if we presume that "tort" means "wrong," "driftway" means "public path, or right-of-way" and "abate" means "to batter down." All of which adds up to the fact that in England they seemingly have public footpaths across private property which go back into the dim and very distant past as to their legality.

Pioneer-day fences in Canada were quite high—five and a half feet being specified in many municipal by-laws. Apparently the early settlers' hungry cattle made short work of low fences. Later on, however, they became lower and lower, until they were little higher than four feet. This is still high enough to keep well-fed cattle securely in or out.

Generally speaking, by-laws were neither strictly enforced nor faithfully obeyed, with the result that they were enacted over and over again. As both labour and materials became scarce fences just became that much skimpier and flimsier. Rails and riders were split thinner, while shorter and slighter stakes were less solidly driven. When the barbed wire fencing age arrived the rail fence had become a mere shadow of its former self and, indeed, was on the way out.

And township councils enacted by-laws dealing with board fences; but these, owing to the increasing cost of lumber and labour, became ever fewer. Stone walls, too, became so scarce that they were seldom referred to, but if well built and sufficiently high, were accepted as legal fences.

In the eighties and nineties of the ninetenth century there was, as may be well imagined, vigorous opposition to barbed wire fences. They were prohibited in some

[ **xxx** ]

towns, and even some rural districts were distinctly hostile. Later on their value as snow fences was discovered and the farmers received a bonus for every rod of wire fence they erected. This is a shining example of how experience outran the law and caused a reversal of legislation.

Of all Canadian provinces, Ontario appears undoubtedly to be the most lavishly fenced. Some of the farms along our main highways of today are cut up into fields almost as small as the fields of southern England. Besides the waste of land, there is the extra time required to cultivate and harvest small fields, and the frequent turning around takes time and is hard on both horses and machinery. Thus it comes about that Ontario is perhaps surfeited with fence legislation. As an instance, the Line Fence Act, the Municipal Act, and the Pounds Act. As line fences gradually were straightened out, and as pioneers and neighbours became more prosperous, and more friendly, too, thank goodness, and as their families grew up, mistakes and disputes were amicably settled, and municipal by-laws and acts of parliament as to fences fell into desuetude.

In pioneer days, what with so much clearing of land, fires were a constant menace to fences. Burning, of course, was the easiest way to dispose of slash, brush and rotten logs. Alexander Wood, a prominent merchant of York (after whose name "Alexander Street" and "Wood Street" were named) in a letter to his client Mrs. Emsley, dated May 23, 1806, tells her how a fire got out of control and menaced the whole neighbourhood, destroying a large part of the lady's fences. Apparently Colonel Shanks, Colonel Smith, Colonel Shaw and Mrs. Givens were also heavy losers.

Needless to say, absentee owners often suffered when neighbours broke down their fences in order to pasture their cattle in some one else's fields. And certainly the Indians had little respect for them, viewing them, as they

[ **xxxi** ]

did, as ready made wood piles, and using them accordingly. When the loyal Canadians were called out to fight the invaders in 1814, the fences, left unguarded, were used by the Indians for their camp fires.

Even when the farms were cleared and Indians and bush fires ceased to be a menace in the settled areas, the snake fence, by reason of the dry rails, weeds and brambles, still remained a fire hazard. Besides, locomotives, steam threshers, tramps and smokers generally were all apt to start fires, and, alas, spite and malice unfortunately cannot be excluded. We all know the careless smoker driving through the countryside even today, so it is astonishing in the long run that so many old time rail and stump fences are still doing duty.

So much for a brief version of the legal end of our Canadian fencing background, including a few of the causes that led to the constant sources of trouble.

### GATES, POSTS AND STILES

Now let us turn to the interesting subject of gates, posts, and stiles, which, in themselves, are an integral part of fences, and walls, and barriers.

Do you recollect the lovely "Lament of the Irish Emigrant" by Selina Sheridan, Lady Dufferin? How haunting and beautiful in its way, it is and always will be:

> I'm sitting on the stile, Mary,
>     Where we sat side by side,
> The corn was springing fresh and green,
>     And the lark sang loud and high,
> And the red was on your lip, Mary,
>     And the love-light in your eye.

Somehow to quote it seems a fitting way to turn our thoughts to the idea of gates, which, dim ages ago, began in the Far East, the cradle of the race, and the original region of walled places and ancient cities. Once "within

[ xxxii ]

the gates" meant one was safe in time of danger. Indeed, to be ordered forth meant excommunication and banishment. Voluntary departure involves high adventure. The poetry of Sion never tires of praising her gates. In a somewhat similar application of the same idea, "dawn came through the gates of day." Spenser, so seldom read now, wrote:

> At last the golden orientall gate
>     Of greatest heaven 'gan to open fayre,
> And Phoebus fresh as bridegroom to his mate
>     Came dancing forth, shaking his dewy hayre,
> And hurled his glistening beams through gloomy ayre.

Many harbour entrances have been called gates, but none is more splendid than San Francisco's magnificent Golden Gate, opening westward.

No fence can be without a gate, for every enclosure must have some means of ingress and egress. In some parts of Ireland, hunters simply knock down and rebuild any particuarly stiff bit of wall, but such rough and ready methods are not at all likely to become general hereabouts.

A gap in a fence is like a breach in a fortification—it makes the rest of the enclosure ineffective. The day once was when city and castle gates were specially designed and constructed because of their military importance. But that is long since past, and now they are preserved largely because of their architectural and ornamental beauty. The magnificent gates of Athens and Rome were the forerunners of Roman triumphal arches.

The farmer's road gate, like the city man's front door, is the face he presents to the world. A warped front door with paint peeling off gives the visitor and passerby an unfavourable impression. In the same way, a sagging and broken gate betrays the shiftless farmer.

Gates were preceded by bars or slip rails. Cows waiting for "Jenny to let the bars down" figure in the poetry of

[xxxiii]

farm life. Where there is much traffic, however, bars entail too great a waste of time and energy in the "letting down" and the "putting up." It is true that "letting down the bars" may be soothing in song, but in practice heavy, warped, ill-fitting bars simply induce profanity and turn young sons and daughters against country life. The "pole-gate," as it is sometimes called, has one great advantage, in that the lower rails may be dispensed with if the owner keeps neither sheep nor pigs, and in time of snow the bars may generally be "left down." The popularity of the pole-gate is, no doubt, mainly due to its cheapness of construction and the improbability of its ever getting out of order. A gate that must be constantly opened and shut in winter entails much snow shovelling and ice chopping—but, with the bars, not so, obviously.

Almost every conceivable type of gate has been shown at the big Ontario exhibitions, and annual rural fairs. The general feeling is that the perfect gate has still to be devised. It would appear that next to effectiveness, then durability, cheapness and simplicity are the decisive factors in determining the farmer's choice.

Hunters and ranchers are noted for their inventiveness and ingenuity in the construction of gates. The chief requirement used to be that gates should be easily opened from horseback. But in the present social arrangement the saddle seems to cut an ever-decreasing amount of ice. It cannot, apparently, hope to hold its own against the airplane, the motor car and motor bike.

Western gates, in Canada, in contrast with those in use in the Eastern provinces are almost always well constructed and non-sagging, and hence are found in good condition, easily opened and closed. Among other ingenious types of Western gates, the level pipe gates for motor cars and trucks (which cattle refuse to cross) are simple and effective, and make transportation easy for the rancher and those who do business with him. Corral gates are a complete study in themselves.

The serviceable swinging gate has always been popular. No gate yet invented, however, satisfies the four conditions laid down by an English writer:

(a) The gate should be self fastening,
(b) When at rest, if possible, it should be sustained by the fastening,
(c) It should be readily opened and shut from horseback, motor vehicle, or on foot,
(d) It should be secure from opening by cattle and other livestock.

We have, ourselves, added the words "motor vehicle" in clause (c), and "and livestock" in clause (d) because they are today so obvious.

The second condition, by far the most desirable for the strength and permanence of the gate, is the hardest of fulfilment. That explains the sagging and twisting of so many farm gates. As for the slip-rail gate, the fastening *is* the gate, which answers a maximum of strength. The gate that fulfils all the conditions seems to be the automatic glass door adopted by many of the chain stores to facilitate the coming and going of customers laden with parcels. The person approaching the door usually breaks a light beam thus setting up the miraculous mechanism which proceeds electronically to open and close the door. Needless to say the same type of device would make the ideal farm gate, but such a thing at present, owing to its cost and its upkeep, is completely out of the question.

Every known method of hinge and fastening has been tried out in rural Ontario. In early years when iron hinges were almost unobtainable several ingenious devices were invented to solve the difficulty. One method was to combine the slip rails in a frame and set one pair of gate posts diagonally. On this pair the gate swung. Although

[ xxxv ]

clumsy, it was easy to construct, required no material but wood, and was solid and effective. However, though once very common, it is, like so many other things, rarely seen today.

A variant of it was the sliding gate, where the slip rail frame was pushed back parallel with the fence. This was good in its way, but rather too heavy for girls and young folk to handle. As farm boys and girls spend a good deal of time opening and closing gates to bring the cattle home for milking, and to let them out afterwards, the clumsy sliding gate was not popular.

With the coming of barbed wire, another makeshift was invented. Wire was fastened to a pair of loose stakes and simply stretched across the opening. When the gate was unlocked it fell in a heap, was dragged to one side, and to close the opening it was dragged back again. The barbs made it awkward and unpleasant to handle, but it was cheap, light and strong.

Gate designs were almost as diversified as those of fences. There were wooden gates of countless sorts, steel frame gates, gates strung with wire, single and double chain gates, and one or two types of cantilever gates operated by counterweights. At the Ontario Provincial Exhibition of 1867 gates manufactured in Peel County were on display. They operated by means of weights which were released when the horse was driven up close and stood on a control platform. This threw the gate open automatically.

Several of the old Ontario counties have very fine examples of ornamental wrought-iron gates. But the one most commonly seen, even on many large estates, is the ordinary four or five barred wooden gate swung on pin and socket hinges. This gate tends to sag, and if the hinges rust or go wrong it takes some strength to drag or pull it open and shut.

Wooden gates harmonize with all kinds of fences, but

iron ones, especially the heavy or wrought kind, are particularly handsome and suitable in combination with stone, brick, or concrete fencing, and, of course, in a hedge or an elaborate wooden fence. A familiar and yet incongruous feature of many Canadian cities and towns is the "residential subdivision" with its imposing sham entrance gateways of stone and iron, often ornamented by carving and grill-work, and the complete absence of any fence whatsoever to which the formal entrance might appertain.

Something similar may be found now and then on a farmhouse, with an elaborate front door, latched and locked, painted and varnished, and set two or three feet above the ground, with no platform nor steps nor other means of approach from the outside, nor any way of egress whatsoever other than jumping. This occurs, we believe, by some saving in taxes to the owner, who insists upon keeping up with the Joneses in actually *having* a front door, even if it isn't usable.

But surely it is the stile that is the most poetic of gates. Lady Dufferin's immortal "Lament" could only have a stile as its background. The singer, of course, might have sat atop a rail fence, but though the seat might have been as secure, it could hardly have been as solid and as comfortable for a young couple. Somehow there just doesn't seem, in our minds, the dignity about sitting on a fence that there appears to be in sitting on a stile. Too many people have fallen off fences, but it is hard to recollect having heard of anyone falling off a stile.

The field stile, of the step or ladder variety, is seldom found in Canada. It is "a set of steps leading over a fence or a wall," and goes with thick hedges and stone walls. Turnstiles, on the contrary, are common in railroad fences and in public paths. Another common stile is a gap with a thick post set in the middle, allowing passage to people, but not to livestock. This is a crude and rather primitive, but effective, form of stile.

Nowadays one seldom meets the "gallows stile," so popular in the 'eighties and 'nineties of the past century. It more usually accompanied a picket fence, and when overgrown with vines and rose bushes it formed a romantic and strikingly beautiful garden ornament.

But enough of stiles for the time being. And let us, too, dispose of another source of fences of an odd and usually sombre nature in as few words as possible. We refer to the cemeteries, and the wide variety of wall, and fence, and barrier that is to be found in the older ones, with their macabre beauty and stateliness with the low walls of stone, surrounding the individual plots. Or stone-capped, with chain from pier to pier. Or wrought iron coupled with marble or granite. How lovely many of them are, but, usually, how pleased we are to be out and away through the massive gateways to our outer, noisy, comfortable seemingly safe mortal world. And the trend in the modern cemetery in Canada, as well as in the United States, appears to be toward the effect of wide, sweeping, well-kept lawns, and away from the small, individual plot with its hard-to-get-at corners for mowing and clipping. Perhaps a lot of the personal and loving touch has been lost in the modern search for monotonous sameness and simplicity of maintenance. And yet there is a strong appeal in the feeling of spaciousness. But let us hurry from cemeteries before the bell tolls and the gates close forever upon us. As is carved around the perimeter of a beautiful granite sun dial in one of the cemeteries we know:

> Hours fly, flowers die,
> New ways pass by,
> *Love stays.*

At least we can remember that, and enjoy its sweetness, and hurry away back to our work, and knitting, and forgetfulness.

# A Summing Up

A casual glance at the old Ontario fences raises many questions in our minds. Were stone fences built to dispose of the piles of field stones, or were the fences really needed? Were stump fences erected because green stumps would not burn? Were snake fences meant as boundaries, to keep farm animals *in* or to keep wild and stray animals *out*?

These and many other questions as simple and yet so difficult to answer come to our thoughts. There was, unquestionably, a vast amount of planning and labour put into the laying out and construction of the old-time barriers. They cost money, and constantly needed repair. They harboured weeds and bushes. They wasted space. They caused snowdrifts that blocked the highways and delayed spring seeding. And they cut up good farms into small fields. But with all their drawbacks they still held many advantages for the yeoman. It should suffice to mention one. An important one to be sure. Ontario, whilst presently giving much attention to soil erosion, has never had to seriously tackle that problem, yet it has caused great havoc in the Canadian West, as well as south of the 49th parallel. Soil erosion. One need hardly say more.

Partly, of course, the Ontario answer is the thicker layer of humus in bush country, but partly, too, the endless number of small fields and their dividing fences which break the force of winds and hold the surface soil on slopes and hills. Ontario farmers have realized the error of taking down their inner fences, and instead of the huge fields they once longed to cultivate and harvest in the Western manner they are now reverting to crop rotation.

A striking and beautiful feature of many an Ontario farm is the number of tall and stately trees. They not only delight the eye, but are a practical and effective windbreak as well. They afford, too, a pleasing shade in summer, and although conifers add cheer to the snows of winter, all are assets of outstanding value. The pioneers who planted them are gone, but they must have been men of foresight, common sense, and good taste. In the Old Land such broad and beautiful avenues of trees usually lead to majestic mansions, where here they lead to snug and well-kept farm homes, to which they lend beauty, adornment and great dignity.

Western Canada is maturing in a different tradition. In early days the ranges were open, but with homesteaders and their type of land development, their livestock has perforce had to be fenced in, while the grain lands, however, are largely at this date unfenced. When a farm is fenced, especially in an exclusively cattle country, boundary fences only are erected. But because of the size of the farms even this entails a vast amount of labour and expense.

The West has dealt in its own way with the fence, the gate and the post problems. Jack pine, not so often found in old Ontario, seems to make the best local post, and if treated with creosote will last well-nigh indefinitely. The dry climate of the West offers good protection against rotting wood. In very dry areas even poplar posts will last a long time.

Under the P.F.R.A. (Prairie Farm Rehabilitation Act) about a million and a quarter acres have been fenced in large blocks. Farmers in these areas use the community pasture system (the fenced-in-fields). Boundary fences are "4 strand wire," with poplar, jack pine, or cedar posts. Interval fences are "3 strand wire," and the corrals are of high poplar or cottonwood poles. Sheep ranches seldom have internal fences.

The Western farmer has to protect his hay while the pasture lasts, so his hay is stacked near his house, and then securely fenced. The rancher's problem involves both summer and winter pastures, and this explains the method, the construction and the location of his fences.

Barbed wire, since it came on the scene, has been popular in the West. When the range is very large, and has little or no internal fencing, it furnishes excellent protection for the stock as well as for the crops. Both cattle and horses dislike it and learn to avoid it, and as the ranges are so extensive this is no hardship.

A word might be in order, too, about brick. The cost of brick fencing in Canada is now so high that it is very seldom used. The necessary foundation carried below frost line, coupled with its maintenance costs because of frost, make it almost an extravagance. Few Canadians have seen a brick wall longer than fifty yards except, perhaps, around public buildings in the older parts of our older cities.

One hundred years ago the farmers often made their own brick on their own farms, and then built good, solid, sensible brick houses, many of which are standing today. Part of the original brick wall which enclosed the grounds of old Beverley House, in Toronto, now occupied by The Ryerson Press, the publishers of this work, is still to be seen on Queen Street, near John Street. A plaque should be put upon it advising of its history.

And speaking of handmade bricks, who can tell exactly where Ontario's first farm was built? It would be as easy to name the first of those artistic stonecutters who utilized stones for farm houses and gateposts. According to John Ross Robertson's *Landmarks of Toronto*, "Springmount," erected in 1830 on Davenport Road near to Dufferin Street, was the first brick house built in York Township. It was built by Bartholomew Bull, the great grandfather of Dr. W. Perkins Bull who collected the material for this book.

Many Canadian firms, even in smaller towns, such as the foundry at Bolton, made iron fences of beauty and dignity. Their work has never received due appreciation. Ornamental fencing is an important architectural feature, and the fences enclosing parks, cemeteries, reservoirs, and public works of all kinds, should be not merely useful but well designed. Men who have raised the standard of craftsmanship have done Canada a real service.

In the 1890's breeders of long-horned Texas cattle experimented with the electric fence. The wild long-horns responded by jumping into the fence about as frequently as away from it. So the electric fence did not come into general farm use until 1932. It is, of course, an amazingly simple fence to construct, consisting of one strand of either barbed or smooth wire, attached to glass or porcelain insulators, on posts or pickets, spaced twenty-to-eighty feet apart, depending on the level of the ground and the class of stock. For average cattle the height of the wire from the ground runs from thirty to thirty-eight inches.

The most widely used fence unit at the present time is the six-volt battery, interrupter, condenser and coil, which transmits a non-lethal but most effective current to the fence line thirty to sixty times each minute. This unit is grounded and attached to the fence line. It will operate five or more miles of fence.

Of course the chief advantage of the electric fence is its low cost, which may be even seventy per cent below that of a standard type fence. The disadvantages are that it may become grounded by growing weeds or grain, which really means it requires occasional patrolling and clearing, or the unit may fail, or become ineffective on dry soil. Animals must be trained to respect an electric fence. Once accustomed to it they will keep carefully away from it and, even though it is not working, will give the single wire and little white bobbin most dutiful attention. It is, somehow, a weird sight seeing a herd of large cows enclosed by a tiny single thread of wire. There is something incongruous about it. Yet there is nearly always one mean critter who will make it her duty to graze within harrowing closeness to it, until at last she touches it, and, finding it is grounded or turned off, wastes no time in pushing her way under it, followed of course, by the balance of the herd all too quickly. Furthermore, one should always bear in mind that it will not stop an infuriated or an excited animal. If you are being chased by a belligerent bull, or an irate cow, don't head for an electric fence at express speed, if there is a good, substantial old-fashioned fence as conveniently at hand. The latter should serve you, if you are fortunate, whereas the former is simply something non-existent as far as your angry pursuer is concerned.

Despite the foregoing limitations, however, the electric fence is presently widely used, and is, apparently, satisfactory for temporary farm fencing.

The chief function of road fences used to be to keep out of one's fields horses, cattle, sheep and pigs running at large, as well as animals pasturing on the roadside, or being driven along the highways. Loose livestock was a serious menace to any other user of a roadway. When automobiles first appeared, conditions, for a time, were even worse. Panic-stricken beasts crashed through fences that were, otherwise, sufficiently substantial, often mangling themselves in the process. Exasperated farmers and irate drovers called down the wildest maledictions on these new devil-wagons, and furiously demanded their abolition. The solution was the motor truck. Now nobody is bothered with livestock on a highway. In these days, instead of tramping long, weary miles to market, fat stock speeds along in big trucks. It is unusual now to see even a hen on the public thoroughfare, even the back concession dirt roads.

To those countless numbers amongst us whose childhood was in part, or in whole, passed on the farm, the fences must always be encrusted as thickly with memories as they were with the berries they gathered in their shade and corners. Who does not remember the wild flowers of yesterday? The nest of the bobolink, and the meadowlark close by? The chittering squirrels racing madly, and wildly, and gracefully along the rails? The rabbits bolting with lolloping ease from their shelter so unexpectedly, and so excitingly? The quail, the partridge, and the pheasant whirling off with loud acclaim from almost underfoot? And the amiable woodchuck ducking swiftly into his burrow amongst the stumps and the boulders?

Even the chores took on a softer, more subdued character with age, and with distance. The sore stone bruises of that barefoot boy are long since healed. The haunting, come-hither flavour of the wild berry remains, whilst the glaring heat and, the cold and the sunburn are gently at last forgotten.

This, then, in brief, is the story of the fences. We like to feel that in some small, remote way this is perhaps the fashion and the format in which it might have been presented to you by those doughty pioneers who devised them.

# FENCES

THIS is undoubtedly one of the first of our North American fences, the palisade surrounding an early Indian village. It clearly shows the heavy supporting posts, and the overlapping, indirect entrance. In case of enemy attack this entrance way could quickly be blocked by heavy cross-logs. The tops of the palisades were charred by fire to point them, to make them harder to get over, and to prevent their decay. The lines of several of these ancient Indian palisades can still be traced in the Huron villages in Simcoe County, in Ontario, Canada, as well as at Fort Ste. Marie, where they were unearthed in excavations carried out by the Royal Ontario Museum. The French enclosed their forts with stockades, for defensive purposes, in the Indian manner, sometimes setting them in earthworks, or dry stone walls.

AN EARLY Indian buffalo pound on the far Western Canadian prairies. It was a form of funnel-shaped stockaded or fenced trap, into whose open end the great beasts were herded by the shouting, gesticulating, war-whooping braves, and thence driven inward to the narrow end where they were quickly dispatched.

The fencing of the pound usually comprised stakes driven into the ground at irregular intervals. Altogether it was an exciting and highly dangerous pastime, but one of the utmost importance, as the buffalo meat was a staple Indian diet. With dried buffalo chips the Indians built fires for cooking and warmth. The hide served for clothing, for tepee shelter, for robes, for blanketing, and for endless other uses, including the travois, that odd vehicle without wheels, devised for dragging loads behind horses.

THE ABORIGINAL FENCE. AN INDIAN BUFFALO

POUND ON THE WESTERN PRAIRIE.

A DEER pound, as pictured in Champlain's *Voyages and Discoveries,* published in 1619. It is probably the "earliest pictorial representation of a Canadian fence . . . its details are obviously erroneous . . . the Indians are too large in proportion to the animals, the trees and the fence . . . the engraver has made the fence much too finished . . . it suggests picketing, sawn and dovetailed together . . . in reality it must have been constructed of rough logs, possibly with branches interwoven among the uprights."

The beaters were apparently using large bones to strike some hollow or flat object, such as a shell or piece of hardwood, to frighten the deer, wolves, foxes and rabbits into the pound, where they were being met at the bottleneck exit by four Indians armed with spears.

A PALISADED Indian village, also from Champlain's *Voyages and Discoveries,* published in 1619. The palisades and platform appear to be built from sawn timber, but this is probably due to the engraver's misunderstanding of Champlain's sketch. Needless to say, only rough hewn logs were used. The figures are far out of proportion, as well as the aggressor's shooting platform, and the Indian longhouses, wherein they lived within the village.

According to Father Gabriel Sagard, there were, above the palisades, in many cases, galleries or watch towers, stocked with stones to hurl down on the enemy, as well as water to put out the fires. Rough ladders led to the towers. The most noticeable lack shown in the drawing is the entire absence of any Indian defenders within the fort itself. To all appearances it seems deserted. Perhaps they have escaped under cover of darkness by canoe on the lake.

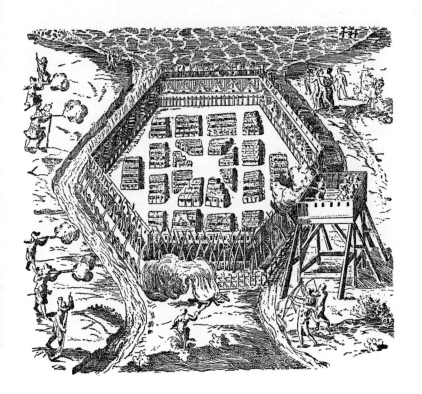

ILLUSTRATING vividly a pioneer logging bee in all its strenuous effort. Four pair of oxen strain every muscle at the cry of the men and the cracking of their whips. The huge stump and roots are on the move. Soon they will be dragged to one side as the land is laboriously torn from the hands of mother nature. Later on, this same stump and roots will probably become part of a fence, amazing in its durability and its effectiveness.

And below we see a typical section of land cleared, with another section beyond the upper fence showing the trees cut down. Good grazing land, but almost useless for the raising of crops. And beyond that, the forest primeval in all its virgin wildness.

A TYPICAL Canadian pioneer log cabin of the early days, in its rough forest clearing. The very earliest settlers cleared garden patches and surrounded them with palisades, the outer pierced with loopholes for shooting. Against the palisades they constructed low log houses, the roofs of which, being lower than the palisades, formed a secondary firing platform. In this way the palisade, the primal North American fence, fulfilled the double function of shelter against the weather and protection against enemies.

The early North West Mounted Police posts were similarly constructed, such as Forts Macleod and Brisebois (Calgary). Such, too, was the plan of the whiskey traders' "posts" whose demoralizing work the "Mounties" broke up. As a general rule no Indian was allowed within the palisade. Trading at Whoop Up, Slide Out and Stand Off was done through narrow openings cut in the logs.

THESE are the stump fences of yesterday, heirlooms from the era of oxen and pioneer. Their sharp silhouette against the sky made a fantastic, antler-like pattern, often beautiful to behold. After the stumping bee they were hauled to the edge of the clearing by the teams of oxen, then turned sidewise and lined up so that the ungainly, tangled roots formed an impenetrable barrier.

The upper picture shows a high stump fence in winter, near Eldorado Park, Peel County, Ontario, Canada.

The lower picture was also made in the same County and at the same season. It is possible that these fences still exist.

B.W.J.

HERE we see the fantastic black and white silhouette of a venerable stump fence. It is an amazing tribute to the artist to have made it so vitally realistic, so sharp and so clear. Evidently it bordered a ploughed field, as three of the furrows show in the foreground. At a glance one can appreciate how impossible it was for livestock to penetrate such a barrier.

The lower drawing shows a magnificent specimen of a pine root in all its complicated detail. To establish its size and majesty the artist has included the figure of a man for comparison. This indeed must have been a giant relic of the virgin stands of timber.

Courtesy of
Professor Eric Arthur

IT WOULD be difficult to find a more impressive and permanent barrier than this, made from mammoth boulders and rough field stones. These, in the days of the settlers of long ago, must have been cleared from the newly won forest land, stone by slow, hazardous stone, and hauled by stolid stone-boat, or rolled heavingly inch by inch to the boundary, with the aid of the straining oxen teams. This splendid drawing depicts accurately an example of this type of fencing which the artist found in Peel County, and includes, to give it proper proportion, a good likeness of Mrs. Hilary Glynn, who presently resides in England. It would seem only fair to add that such a fence would rarely be found in Canada.

Courtesy of
Professor Eric Arthur

THESE two drawings show superb examples of an old-time, dry stone fence, on the Kirkwood Farm, Lot 5, Concession 4, in the Township of Caledon. Like the fence on the preceding page it was built of boulders and field stones cleared from the adjoining fields, but is different and more costly in that the individual stones of varying size were shaped and dressed with mallet and chisel so as to lock neatly and securely together without mortar. Such fencing required no foundation carried below frost level, and moved gently with the movement of the land upon which it stood.

The artist has included in the upper drawing his co-worker and contemporary, Dr. W. Perkins Bull.

THIS nice example of a solid and well-built stone wall must share the honours with the then young Bob Haggert, Brampton, Ontario. The date was 1871, and he was the star baseball player for the rather recently formed Maple Leafs, who in that year played its first series of baseball games with the neighbouring towns.

THIS very odd-looking fence arrived in Canada with the advent of saw mills, and was commonly known as a sawyer's fence. It was supported by crossed stakes driven firmly into the ground. Mostly it was found built near one of the old saw mills, where rough slabs of wood and discarded planks were often thrown out as being of little use. At that time wood was in great abundance and the cost was low.

THE old frame Meeting-House of the early nineteenth century in the village of York, which later became Toronto. Picket fences and rough plank sidewalks were in vogue then, and the roads were—well, just nice old mud, dirt and dust roads.

AFTER the brush and root fences came the log fences fresh from the forests cleared to supply the land for plough and seed. The logs were sixty feet long, as shown in the upper drawing, by two and a half feet thick at their butts supported on transverse sleepers, held together by stout caps and stakes, and alternating heavy and light ends. Boulders under the bottom logs kept them off the ground and dry, thus slowing decay.

The lower illustration gives a different treatment, with uniform, cut logs of only sixteen feet, and with a straight run, one upon another, with two stakes about five feet high driven well down on either side, where these light logs overlapped. As time passed, the panel, or length, was reduced from sixteen to twelve feet, as being an easier length for one man to handle. Without caps or wire the stakes, no matter how well driven were almost sure to spread at the top given time and the impulsive cow.

HERE is a case of sixty-foot logs simply being placed skilfully one on top of the other, regardless of their not being entirely straight, and forming a formidable fence. The great weight of such logs played the determining factor in their usefulness and success.

The lower drawing shows a log barrier that is defective because the material is too warped and crooked. Such fences encourage livestock to put their heads through the openings to graze on the other side, which leads to their throwing off the top log and then proceeding over the fence followed by the entire herd. Many a good pioneer squabble has arisen through such circumstances.

THIS is an excellent example of a sturdy, well-built log fence. The bottom log is the thickest, whilst the others diminish in size to a narrow topmost member. The logs are supported by transverse sleepers, and the fence is held firmly together by well-driven upright stakes, and bored caps. Such a fence made good neighbours.

In comparison to the above, the fence in the lower picture shows many faults, and was probably a trouble maker. The upper logs will allow the cattle to squeeze their heads through. The logs are too varying in size. There are no proper transverse sleepers. And the stakes are badly driven, and wired shakily together at the top.

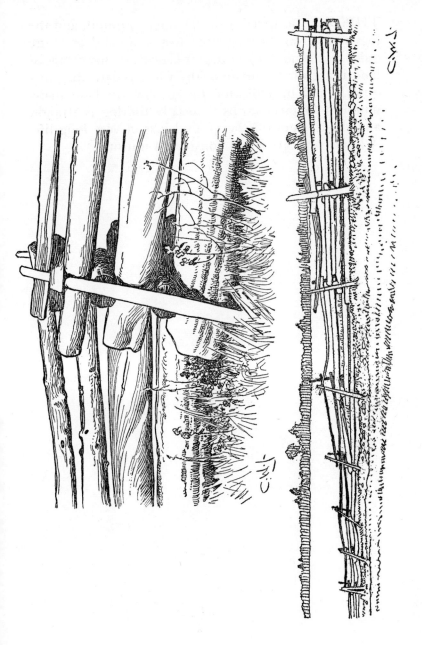

THIS fence occurred in low, swampy ground, and the logs were from fifty to sixty feet long, and of white cedar indigenous to Ontario, Canada. Boggy, moist land is a great favourite of the white cedar. It grows quickly and in profusion on the low land on many southern Ontario farms. Usually the log is straight and slim. Kept off the ground it is of very long life. A hundred years is not considered unusual.

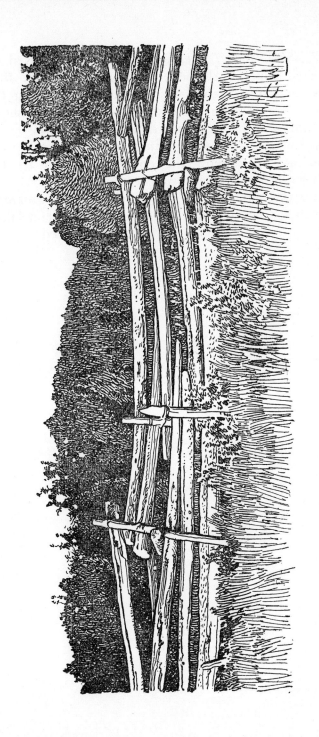

OCCASIONALLY the fence logs were grooved or notched for the sleepers, as illustrated here, thus making a snugger and tighter fit, and bringing the logs desirably closer together. Also it clearly shows the hole for the stake bored through the end of the log. Incidentally, as a specimen of craftsmanship the drawing, like almost the entire collection by Dr. Jefferys, leaves little to be desired.

Below is an individual drawing of a transverse sleeper, or cap, bored with three inch diameter auger holes to receive the stakes already mentioned.

THE left hand drawing shows a log fence whose logs and sleeper-ends have become so rotted that it will be necessary to dismantle the fence, bay by bay, cut the logs shorter individually, create new sleepers or caps, and rebuild the entire fence in the shorter logs, and probably with new stakes as well.

The other two illustrations depict other log fences of similar construction and were like the ones on pages fifteen and seventeen, drawn in meticulous and loving detail by Dr. Jefferys, in Peel County, Ontario, Canada.

ANOTHER splendid example of a log fence of the very definitely bull-nay order, with transverse sleepers and stakes. A sturdy barrier to be sure, and one that the crinkly-horned, bad-tempered cow might just as well forgo.

STILL another interesting treatment of the end of a pioneering log fence, showing the bottom member resting on stone, and stones reinforcing the transverse sleepers and weighing them down in place, as opposed to the more arduous method of boring auger holes and driving vertical stakes. Note how the ends of these particular logs are rapidly decaying, which will mean arduous rebuilding.

A CAREFULLY-BUILT, staunch log fence, with the log ends resting on each other, and supported by stout stakes driven deeply, but with no transverse sleepers. The stakes were renewed from time to time. The height was about six feet, as borne out by the figure of the farmer in overalls.

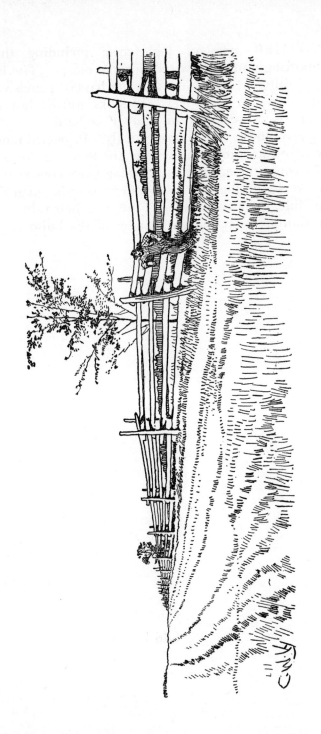

ANOTHER type of log fence, including thick supporting posts, and wired in some places. The logs are of different lengths so that the bays or panels vary from thirty to forty feet. It looks sturdy, but the wiring is a weakness in that it is hard to secure properly, and it rusts out so quickly. If joggled much, the wire eats into the wood and the logs then loosen.

As you can see, the variety of log fence construction was very considerable, dependent on the materials available, their availability to the site, their value, and the thoroughness and enthusiasm of the builder.

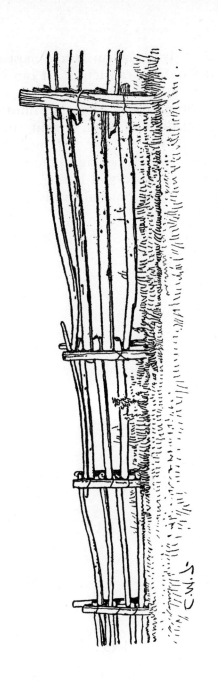

ONE of the early Canadian fences most popular in the east was the snake rail fence. It can still be seen here and there in the rural sections. It was built in a variety of forms, as the following illustrations will show. It was made from poles, or split rails, the latter being usually of white cedar. If made from poles, then black ash, hickory, oak and pine were favourites because they were tough and lasting. In rolling and broken country it was a prime favourite because of its adaptability.

C.W.J.

A TYPICAL six rail snake fence, of split rails and narrow logs of varying length, but approaching uniformity, with their ends resting on each other, and without stakes. The difference in the rail lengths made an insecure barrier, as the intersection of the rails assumed an incline instead of an upright centre of weight. The top rails, of course, were forever getting knocked off, with the inevitable result that in time the livestock moved in on someone else's crops.

AN EARLY snake fence made out of rails, with the ends resting on each other, and braced at each angle, or bay, by two upright stakes, one on either side of the fence, driven well into the ground, and tightly wired together at the top to support the upper rails, as well as to keep the tops of the stakes in steady position. The bottom rail, in alternative bays, rested upon the ground, thus being soon rotted out through continual dampness. One of Canada's most picturesque institutions, the snake fence was, and still is, widely known in the United States as well. It has been suggested that it originated in Virginia, but no definite evidence supports this theory.

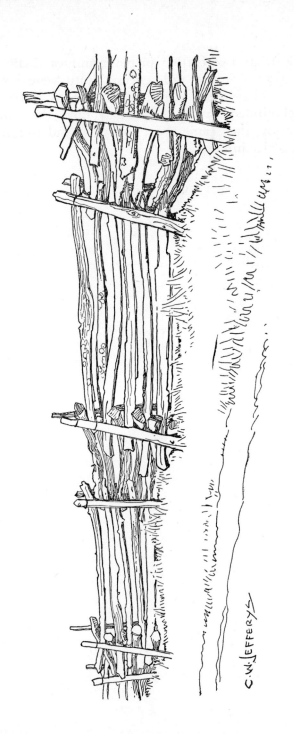

C.W. JEFFERYS

THESE are two further prime examples of the snake type split rail and rail fences. Both were six rails high. They were fairly vulnerable to those more travel-minded cattle. For small boys they were a sheer joy, they came apart so easily, and tumbled in such a nice jumble.

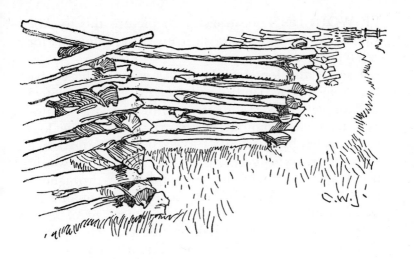

IT WOULDN'T be difficult to picture this as Abe Lincoln as a young man, splitting a log into rails for rail fencing.

Usually the logs being split were, roughly, twelve feet long, by two and a half feet in diameter. Steel wedges were driven into them with what was known as a heavy, iron-bound beetle, as shown. The logs were preferably straight, and each one would make three, four, six or even eight rails. Good rails would be of approximately the same thickness throughout their length. The split was started at the small end, then a wedge would be inserted, of steel, or of some hard wood such as white oak or hickory. The splitter then followed along the median line to keep the split true from end to end. Sometimes it took two wedges only, but three or four were really better. It needed great skill to avoid splintering, and an inexperienced hand would waste both time and logs. White cedar, indigenous to Ontario, made the best rails. Some are still to be seen in the rural areas, having long ago outlived their makers.

IN THE upper drawing is a straight rail fence, not split, with stakes, one on either side, with no wiring. And the stakes are not a split rail either. The stakes must have been carefully and deeply driven, and the rails with approximately the same end sizes, or the fence would easily have collapsed.

The second drawing is of a typical, good, old-fashioned snake fence, with the rails split and merely piled one upon another, without stakes or wire. Those breachy type cattle soon discovered the possibility in the loose upper rails, and soon the whole herd was grazing over yonder in old Will's alfalfa, where they rightly shouldn't be, dang 'em.

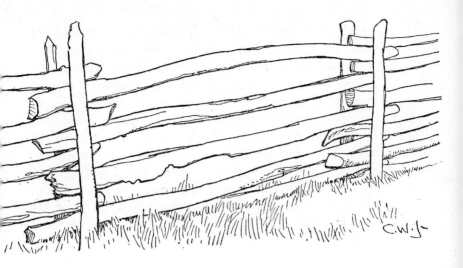

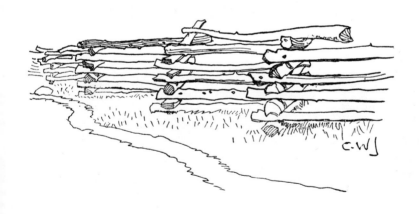

HERE we have a straight rail fence, not split, and not snake, showing the supporting stake driven deeply in on one side only and to which the rails are wired.

The lower drawing is different again, being a straight split rail fence with stakes driven deeply about a rail width apart at the overlapping junctions, the split rails being laid between the stakes from the ground up, and resting on each other. No wire was used, and the stakes were at about ten foot intervals. In this case the stake was apparently stouter and of split rail, with the lower end sharpened. The stakes must have been thoroughly rigid or the whole fence would have collapsed.

All drawings, with few exceptions were, of course, of fences actually existing in the era from 1935 to 1940 and were undertaken in the field by Dr. Jefferys.

THIS is that amazing old billy goat you have already read about, belonging to Dr. Jim McKay, of Elmbank, in the County of Peel, Ontario, Canada, picking his way circumspectly homeward along the top of the rail fence after his daily visit to Button's Tavern at the Claireville five corners, where he had, as usual, joined the local boys in a glass or so of not so mild refreshment. From the expressions on his admirers' faces old billy was finding the going a little treacherous.

AND now comes the next type of early pioneer fencing, the log and stone fence, in its various forms. Having cleared the fields of boulders the settler sometimes found them not enough, so turning to his stand of wood, he cut down and used logs, as shown, to top off the necessary height. In this case transverse sleepers and well-driven stakes through the sleepers completed a barrier of excellent efficiency and durability.

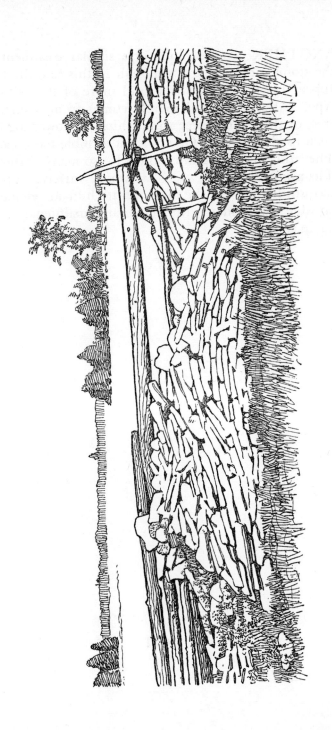

ANOTHER good example of a similar treatment of the stone and log fence, although in this case the logs appear lighter, and shorter, and more of the rail-size type. After all, a rail merely comes from a smaller tree, or the top of a tree from which the lower log has been used otherwise. One mustn't quibble too greatly. The study of fencing must allow for so many normally unconsidered items such as wood variety, supply accessibility, cost, the important human element, possible uses and requirements, and maintenance—to name a few.

IN EASTERN CANADA, at least, no country fence would seem complete without its chattering, dancing, racing, scolding, friendly, inquisitive family of squirrels. Here is a typical summer scene. Papa and Mama black squirrel sitting as bold as brass in front of our very noses. Mama is eating a nut, or washing her face, whilst Papa is swearing, and chittering, and scolding the artist.

HERE we have a log and stone fence of still another kind, being of the zigzag, or snake order, with the rails resting one upon another for stability. At about ten foot intervals two inclined stakes were well planted, with their butts about three feet, or more apart. These stakes intersected one another above the third or fourth rail, and supported a topmost rail. It was mostly constructed of whole logs, or rails, rather than Abraham Lincoln's split rails.

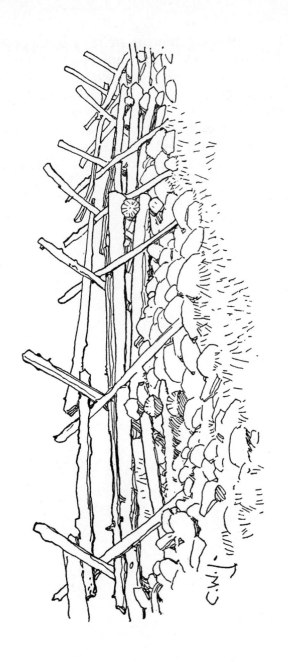

IN THE left-hand drawing we see a well-put-together log and stone fence, with transverse sleepers, but no stakes. A good barrier, but without stakes the topmost member remains vulnerable to that cow with the crinkled horn.

The right hand shows a rail and stone job, with posts driven deeply and wired together below the top rail. The wire often ended up by sagging or stretching, and then old Will was at loggerheads with Ephraim all over again.

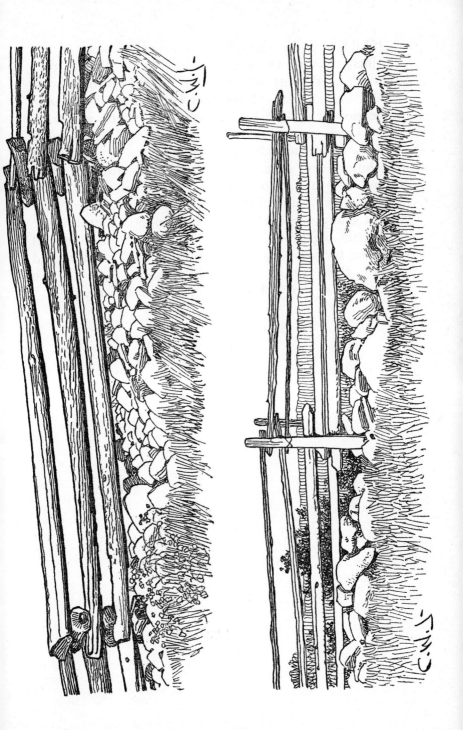

HERE are the once famous Fence Viewers of the olden days in Ontario, Canada. Very British they seem, by the cut of their clothing, their sturdy boots and beaver hats. Important custodians of a goodly portion of the local peace of mind. Their power, as we know, was *very* considerable indeed. They could, without further ado, force young Zeke to rebuild his whole fence, or any part thereof, dictating of what and how it was to be built, and just precisely when young Zeke must finish it. The particular fence they are examining and discussing does not appear to be exactly pig proof, and it is likely its rebuilding will make for good neighbourliness. Good citizens, and fair, these Fence Viewers of the long ago. At two dollars per day each they did not seem lavishly paid.

Fence Viewers

C.W.JEFFERYS

THESE two drawings further illustrate rail and stone fences, resting their ends on transverse sleepers, and with intersecting stakes set at an angle, with their butts braced amongst the boulders. Such fences were more often found in rough and broken country.

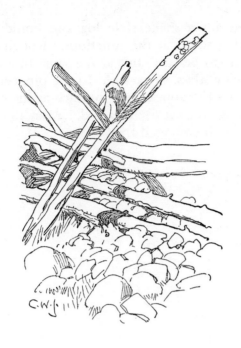

THIS time it's a snake style log and boulder fence with slanting stakes at the junctions. Rough enough it does look, to be sure, but at the same time rugged, and thus, doubtless, successful. In the pioneer days it wasn't always the appearance so much as the effectiveness of things that really counted. Even the look of it must have discouraged the livestock.

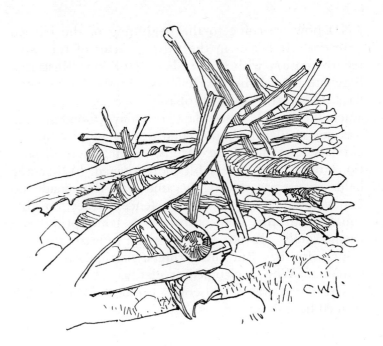

AND now we come to the beginning of the barbed wire era. It began in the third quarter of the nineteenth century with the crude type of wire illustrated herewith so well by Dr. Jefferys. In those long gone days the cattle were probably not as docile and amenable as their descendants of today. Good grazing was not so plentiful, and conditions generally for the animals were not so luxurious, so that their dispositions, doubtless, were a bit more rugged. When the fields they were grazing became lean they made no bones about going through a fence if they possibly could. But this new barbed wire contraption tore them cruelly. It took time for them to learn a proper respect for it. But the farmers, particularly in the Canadian West, welcomed it gladly. Where timber was scarce it was a godsend. From 1873 onward it seemed here to stay.

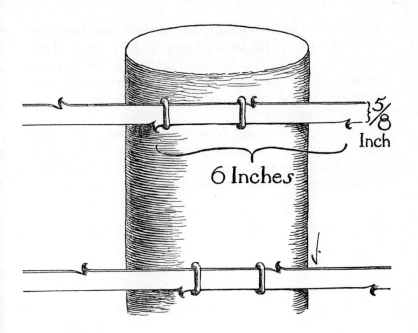

NOW we go back to the log and stone fences, but with the addition of this new-fangled barbed wire. This means the fences can be lower as far as the logs are concerned, and then the barbed wire (which has now advanced to the more modern style) strung above it from stake to stake.

The upper drawing is of that log and stone type, with the stakes driven diagonally, whilst the other is of the kind that used transverse sleepers, but with the log and not the sleeper bored to take the stake.

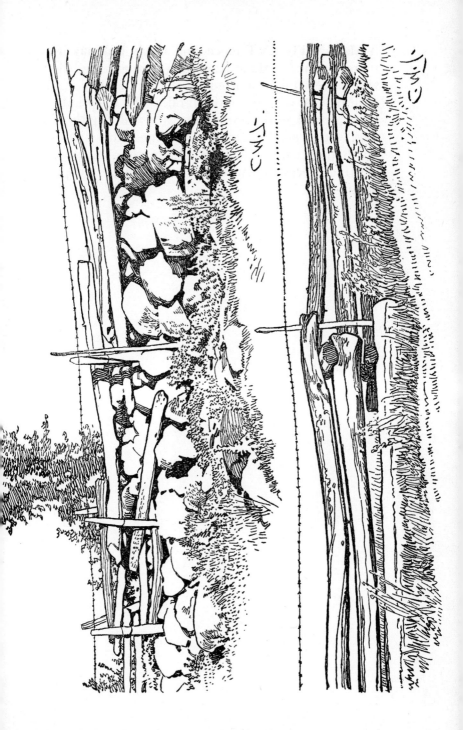

A MAGNIFICENT fence, and surely bull-nay if ever there was one. Made from long, straight logs, bound with wire, and supported by sleepers and stakes and with barbed wire to top it all off. The telegraph pole gives a good indication of the size and length of the logs. It is needless to say that these drawings were not figments of the artist's imagination, but were of existing fences drawn to the most careful and precise detail.

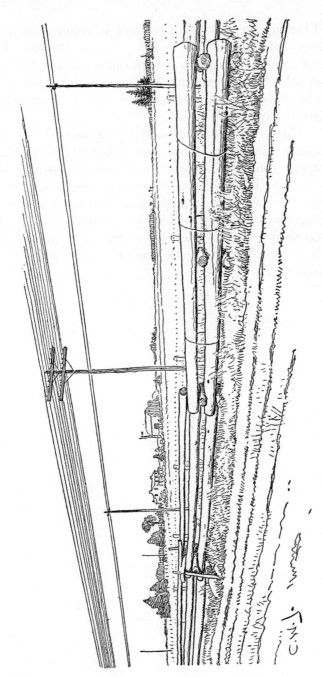

F—5

THE upper shows a neat and effective wire garden fence, fastened to its round posts by staples. It was not a cheap fence, but it kept out smaller animals such as rabbits and ground hogs, which otherwise played hob with those cabbages and the lettuce and delicious green peas.

The lower drawing illustrates a barbed wire fence, where the lower strands are closer together than the upper ones. The base comprises an upright board, one foot in width, nailed to the posts and extending two posts, whilst a top board of a similar nature, slightly slanted, is nailed to the post tops, its joints occurring at two post intervals, alternative with the base board. This fence was expensive and took time and care to build.

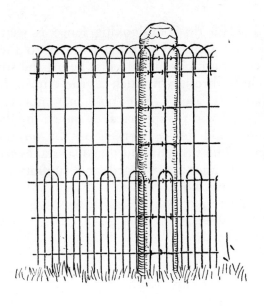

SOMETIMES this odd-looking fence is seen in the more barren Ontario farming country to the north, where rock outcroppings lie just below the surface or break clean through it, such as the approach to the Georgian Bay area. The post may not enter the ground at all and is supported, as shown, by the clever rock and wood device worked out by our forebears long ago. The upright and diagonal stakes are nailed to the post, and are wedged and supported by the carefully placed boulders.

A MODERN kind of barrier known as a seven-strand wire fence, topped off with barbed wire. There are, as you will note, seven horizontal strands of wire, wider apart as they leave the ground, hence its name of seven-strand. To be really effective the wire should be stretched and held tautly between posts. The barbed wire discourages hunters as well as animals and the best way to get over it is to go around it.

The lower drawing shows a similar style of fence to the upper but it uses growing trees as opposed to posts. It, of course, presupposes that the trees are evenly spaced, in a straight line, and more or less uniform in size and shape.

Barbed wire now comes in various wire thickness and weight, and strand fences may be purchased in varying height, and numbers of strands.

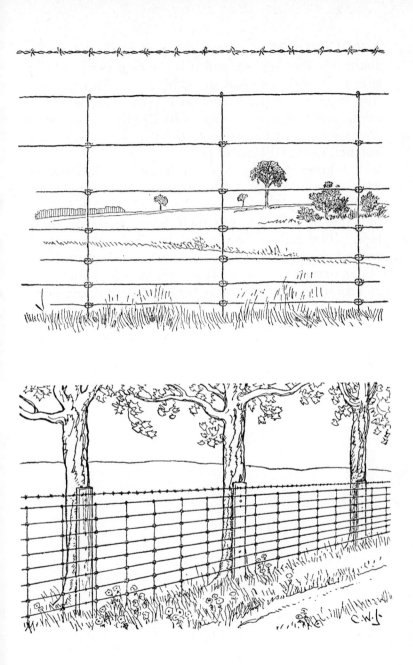

A ROUGH-HEWN oaken gate post of the long ago, about one foot square, and still showing marks of the adze or broad axe used in shaping it. Also the old iron supports of the hinges set deeply into the tough wood, and the upper hinge still hanging dejectedly. The gateway no longer used, the wire fence has been fastened to the still useful post.

The lower drawing depicts a fence of plain barbless wire, six strands, stapled to the posts, and topped with barbed wire. The corner posts were cleverly braced by squared rails set into their bases and near their tops. The rails were secured by thick wire looped around them midway of their length, and around the upper part of the posts. It was tightened by inserting and rotating a stick midway between the rail and post.

THESE were often the gates and fences of the Canadian West, made from poles and therefore known by that name. Jack pine or cedar or even poplar was used. But with the scarcity of wood on the prairies the advent of wire was a true godsend. Remark the care with which the gate was made, and the cross bar to keep it from sagging, and the type of stout metal hinges and fasteners. The latter defied the best efforts of the livestock to open.

As will be seen, the poles of the fence were nailed to the posts in alternating fashion for rigidity.

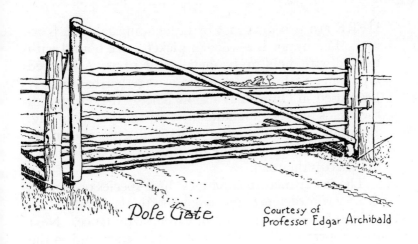

Pole Gate

Courtesy of
Professor Edgar Archibald

Pole Fence
for live stock Corral

Courtesy of
Prof. Edgar Archibald

HERE are two drawings of rather unusual-style fencing. The upper is a wooden picket fence bound with twisted wire, held up by metal angle irons. A kindred type fence with the pickets closer together has latterly been used in Ontario as a snow fence. It is erected in the fields in the fall and dismantled in the spring, alongside the highways where drifting formerly occurred, and sets up the drifting in the field, rather than across the road.

The lower picture combines three species of fencing in one run of fence and seems particularly odd. To the left is shown a section of garden wire fence. Next to it appears a short stretch of picket fence, and to the right a horizontal board fence with two-inch flat stakes nailing the boards on the outside of the fence. We have no explanation for this unusual admixture, as the original drawing with the usual careful notations by the artist is missing in this one, lone instance.

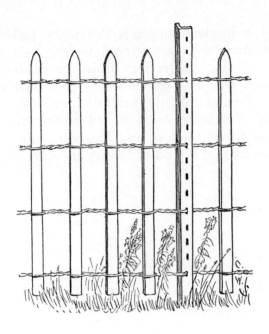

WHAT a lovely example is this white picket fence and wooden post, surmounted by the well proportioned ball cap. It breathes of the Victorian era, and of elegant and truly gracious living, of lovely ladies in crinolines, and dainty, brightly hued silk sunshade parasols, of dancing, foam-flecked horses, and surreys with the fringe on top, and laughter, and gentility, and courage and a kind of beauty and easy elegance.

ANOTHER, but less ornate picket fence, posts, and gate leading into the front garden. The pickets were nailed to scantlings which rested on top of the posts set on the inner side of the fence. Along the line of the scantlings, in front of the pickets, a horizontal wooden slat was nailed, whilst a moulded base board was set in front against the bottom of the pickets. The gate pickets cleared the ground, and were nailed to horizontal upper and lower bars, with a diagonal bar bracing the whole. A sturdy enough fence and one which the boys and girls were forever climbing over and getting their clothes caught on in devastating fashion. Remember?

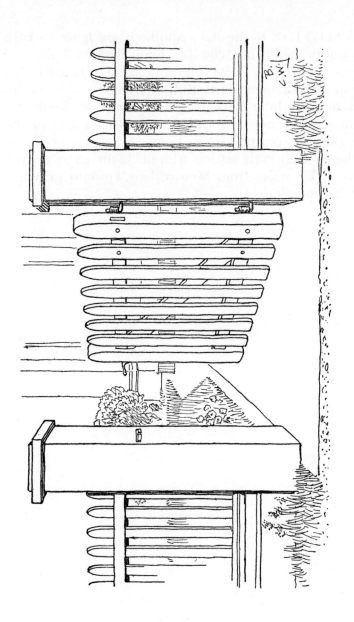

A SECTION of the Balquahollie board fence in York County, built in 1866 by John Perkins Bull, and given by him with its fine, commanding house to his son Bartholomew Hill Bull, on the occasion of his wedding. John Perkins' grandfather, old Bartley as he was affectionately called, came to Canada in the eighteenth century from Tipperary, and was one of those sturdy early settlers who made their way on foot some 350 miles from Montreal to Toronto to homestead and pioneer.

HISTORY abounds with hedges in most countries. Here is a Canadian black thorn, a lovely, dishevelled but effective barrier, which, like white cedar, hawthorn, locust and box, may be occasionally found in Ontario. In England it is hawthorn and wild rose, or clipped and sophisticated beach, yew, privet, box and holly. In New Zealand it's gorse; in the Isle of Man, beautiful fuchsia; cactus in California, and laurel and holly in British Columbia.

NEXT come the ornamental iron fences. Beautiful things they are and were, but far too expensive for the average purse. More usually they were found around public buildings and gardens or churches, or in cemeteries. The one herewith shown is a classic example, and clearly illustrates the adornment and the detail. The magnificent iron fence around Osgoode Hall, in Toronto, already mentioned, has one most notable feature—its gates. These are of very odd and interesting design, being in a sense rather like stationary revolving doors. And can you guess why they were so constructed? To keep the cows out!

C.W.J

Courtesy of Professor Eric Arthur

AND now we come to the gateways of the past, the present, and perhaps the future.

This cast iron gate is of rose and lily pattern and was to be seen in the town of Bolton, in Peel County, Ontario, where it was cast. It was a fine example of this rapidly vanishing type of work.

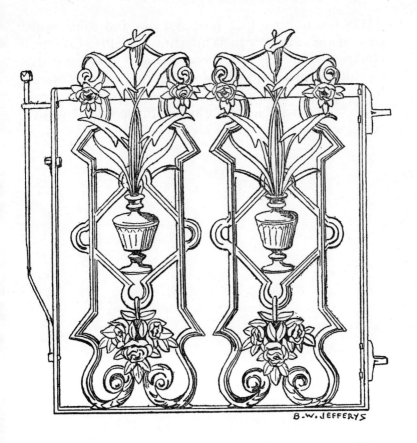

B. W. JEFFERYS

THIS lovely stone gate post and cap and stone wall were at the cemetery in Whitechurch in Peel County, Ontario. The neighbourhood was well known for its carefully constructed dry stone fences, and doubtless this excellent example of craftsmanship was undertaken away back in the nineteenth century by the selfsame Scotch immigrant mason.

AN INTERESTING collection of early homemade Canadiana in the form of a mill stone, stone gate post, pole fence, and pole gate, found at Millburn's Allandale Mills, in County Peel. They were rugged, yet forthright, and the pole gate was a thing of real beauty.

THESE impressive field stone gateposts were assembled and built by Robert G. Logan on his farm near Mount Wolfe, Lot 23, Concession 9, Albion Township, in Peel. Somehow the wire gate seems disappointing by comparison. Doubtless the original gates were of wood, and perhaps more picturesque.

The lower drawing is of a well-finished wooden gate in Western Canada, on some ranch and horse corral. Note the cross-bracing and the long, sturdy strap hinges. The latch, of wood, is of the type that even a wily bronco could not open.

C.W. JEFFERYS

Gate for Horse Corral    Courtesy of Professor Edgar Archibald

THE olden day toll gates! What fascinating things they were for those of us who can still recollect them. But how they must have been abhorred by our grandparents.

Here we see the Dundas Street Toll House, as it was known, in all its simple wooden dignity. On its wall for all travellers to see hung the sign, like the one printed below, outlining the tolls to be collected. "Vehicle drawn by two horses or other cattle — 6 pence." And dated New Year's Day, 1851. All have gone long since. Now it is motor cars and aeroplanes.

UNDER THE AUTHORITY
of
PARLIAMENT
The Gore and Vaughan Plank Road
rate of Tolls to be collected thereon
for each time passing whether loaded
or otherwise

|  | £ | s | d |
|---|---|---|---|
| for every Vehicle drawn by two Horses or other Cattle | 0 | 0 | 6 |
| for every additional horse or beast | 0 | 0 | 2 |
| " " Vehicle drawn by one horse | 0 | 0 | 3 |
| " " Horse Ass or Mule | 0 | 0 | 2 |
| " " score of Neat Cattle | 0 | 0 | 1 |
| " " score of Sheep or Swine | 0 | 0 | 1 |

By orders of the Directors

Dated Jan[uar]y 1851

F—6

TWO more Ontario toll gates of interest. The upper one seems of a more advanced and well-planned type with its sheltering roof for the wayfarer as he got out his purse and paid the shot. Note the small receiving window to the right of the doorway. Doubtless it was used at night, thus saving dressing and going outside. The lower toll gate was at Brockton (Parkdale, Toronto) and shows a typical winter scene of the times, three creaking sleigh loads of wood.

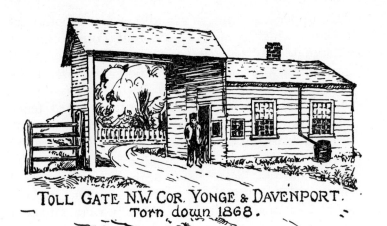

TOLL GATE N.W. COR. YONGE & DAVENPORT.
Torn down 1868.

THE upper drawing shows the old post office at Brockton, which became a suburb of Toronto known as Parkdale, and later became part of the city itself. The earliest known date of the post office was 1855. It is an interesting period piece, with the sunflowers showing over the top of the horizontal board fence and the long dress of the woman depicted trailing the mud and dirt from the path, as was then the unhealthy custom.

Below is St. James Church, Caledon East, Peel County, illustrating three types of fencing, and the gate. The carriage sheds to the left were almost a church necessity in those days, and a few may still be seen about the Canadian countryside.

A RATHER complicated but interesting gate from the days of the horse and the surrey with the fringe on top. It was self opening but apparently not self closing. When the buggy wheel struck the vertical trip it was pressed down into the box, throwing the rod which lifts the upper hinge backward, allowing the gate to swing open, which, being so hinged, it did on being unlatched. Note the turned gate posts and caps, and the special picket fence. It all bespoke an owner of means. But even that might not make it work in winter.

The lower drawing is self explanatory and shows a neat latching device for a wooden gate. Unhappily most such conveniences were usually less practical than ornamental, and needed constant adjustment and repair.

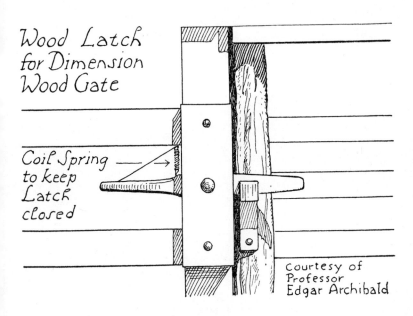

**Wood Latch for Dimension Wood Gate**

Coil Spring to keep Latch closed

Courtesy of Professor Edgar Archibald

A SURPRISING carpentry achievement of the last century, showing a neat and well constructed pair of wooden posts and caps, with moulded panels, all fastened stoutly together with wooden pegs and hand wrought, square-headed nails. The fence and gate were closed deeply at the base with wide boarding to keep out small animals from the gardens and flower beds, whilst the whole was surmounted with a narrow, slanting board to keep off the moisture.

Painted, and well maintained, and not backed into by trucks and small boys too often, it would outlive most of us.

C.W. JEFFERYS

Detail
of
Construction
of
Fence

THESE fence posts show originality and pleasant design. The cast iron post was a favourite in its day, and was usually painted a gay and lively green. It was a city or town dweller, of course, and has, all too sadly, almost disappeared.

All in all, fence posts often show great ingenuity of design, as in the case of the wooden ones illustrated. The four upper, graceful specimens are tops of turned wood on solid, round posts. The lower one makes use of a solid urn or vase motif as a finial set upon the projecting cap of a square or boxed post.

Cast Iron
Fence Post

Wooden Fence
Posts

THE upper figures show a gatepost and the upright post of the gate itself, and illustrates the old-fashioned iron hinge idea. Both members, as can be seen by the dotted lines, ran right through the posts in drill holes.

The latching device matched the hinges, and was also made by the blacksmith from ¾" round iron bars. It was a good, sensible, durable type of latch.

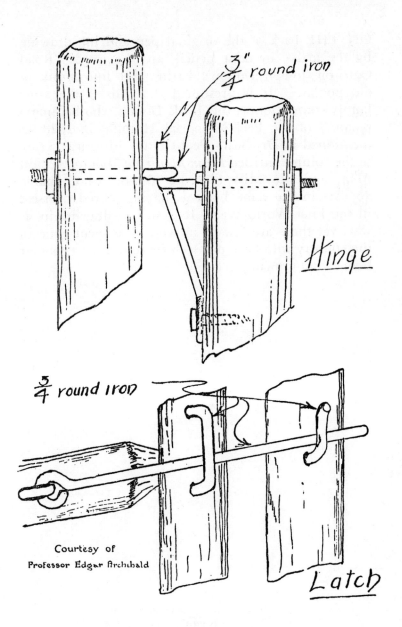

$\frac{3}{4}$" round iron

*Hinge*

$\frac{3}{4}$ round iron

Courtesy of
Professor Edgar Archibald

*Latch*

ON THE back of the original pen and ink drawing by the artist, in faint pencil, are the words "Road Gate on Joseph Dolson's Farm. Set into trunk of old poplar." It is presumed that this is the same family connection as the J. M. Dolson who became a member of the Peel Memorial Hospital in 1928, as mentioned in Dr. Bull's Peel County historical series, in the volume entitled *From Medicine Man to Medical Man,* and the Miss Florence Dolson whose name appears in the same book as having served overseas in the First World War. It is an odd drawing in its way, yet there are few of us who have spent time in the country who have not seen its counterpart, poplar being a fast-growing tree.

THESE three illustrations are fairly self-explanatory, and serve to show ingenious pasture gateways that the lowing herd could not navigate successfully. The common turnstile was simple and sturdy, whilst the fence gap turning parallel to the main fence, and with its narrowness, was effective, other than for small calves.

The wheel turnstile with the tire chains drooping therefrom was distinctly more so, but something will have to replace those tire chains, as they are no longer in use.

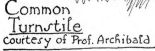

Common
Turnstile
courtesy of Prof. Archibald

Fence Gap, narrow enough
to prevent horses and cattle
from getting through

Wheel Turnstile, made from
old drill wheel, with alternate
spokes cut off. Old tire
chains attached to turn
small live stock.

THIS illustration of chain gates is a most amazing and curious item and shows a type of gate one would never hope to see today. On the other hand, the more one studies it the more one can see the possibilities of the novelty. Simply throwing over the self-locking lever drops the whole affair to the road.

The double-chain gate at the bottom in theory appears a mite more complicated, although in practice it may not work out that way. The seeming lowness of both barriers appears surprising.

# Chain Gates

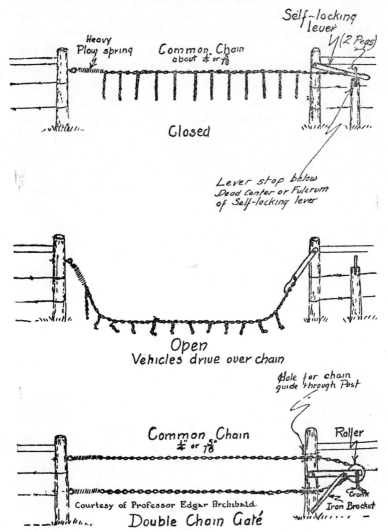

Self-locking lever
V (2 Pegs)

Heavy Plow spring

Common Chain about ¾ or ⅞

Closed

Lever stop below Dead Center or Fulcrum of Self-locking lever

Open
Vehicles drive over chain

Hole for chain guide through Post

Common Chain ¾ or ⅝"

Roller

Crank

Iron Bracket

Courtesy of Professor Edgar Archibald.
Double Chain Gate

IF YOU care for crossword puzzles this novel gate should be more than usually interesting. It takes the average observer quite a time to figure out how the thing works. To operate it, we would suggest lifting the two-bar gate and moving it to the left, until the vertical brace joining the two bars (shown about two inches from the left-hand gate post) strikes the lower or inner gate post. This will then clear the gate from the right, and permit it to be carried out of the way, where, in its open position, it will rest on the vertical upright illustrated about one inch in the drawing from the lower gate post. The whole thing is ingenious, and if well built of strong light weight material should serve most effectively.

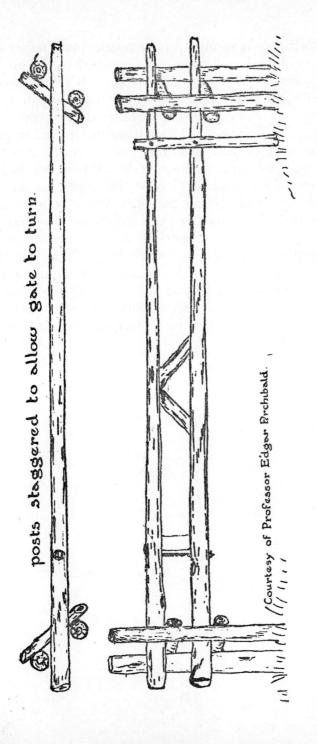

posts staggered to allow gate to turn.

(Courtesy of Professor Edgar Archibald.)

AND here is another proper puzzle. It is rather more complicated and somewhat fancier than the one just discussed. Actually what happens is that a two bar pole gate is pivoted by a strong bolt through a short log, and through the two right-hand gate posts. This acts as a hinge for the gate to swing upward upon. A short log of heavy wood is attached to the two right-hand gate posts by iron rods. When this is lifted upward and over to increase the weight on the right end of the upper gate pole (the whole being adjusted so that the gravel in the buckets permits just nice balance when the gate is down) the entire gate cantilevers upward into a vertical position, out of the way. The bucket of gravel acting as counter balance somehow adds a bizarre touch. It is presumed that the bucket has holes in its bottom to allow rain water to escape; either that or a cover against both rain and snow.

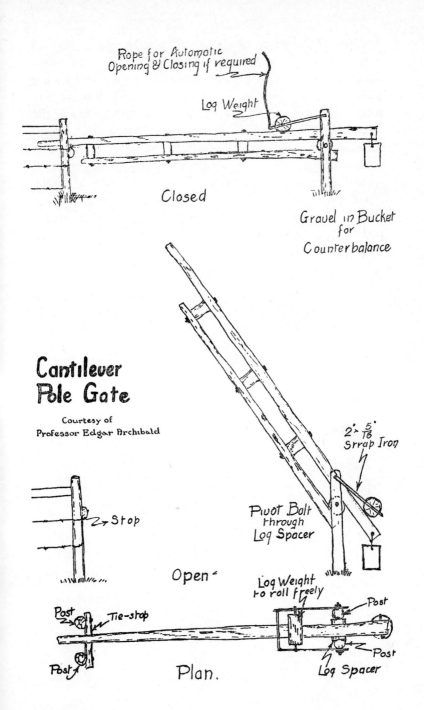

Rope for Automatic
Opening & Closing if required

Log Weight

Closed

Grauel in Bucket
for
Counterbalance

Cantilever
Pole Gate

Courtesy of
Professor Edgar Archibald

2" 5"/16
Strap Iron

Pivot Bolt
through
Log Spacer

Stop

Open

Log Weight
to roll freely

Post

Tie-stop

Post

Post

Post

Log Spacer

Plan.

A GOOD looking modern farm gate made out of 2 x 4's with a sensible kind of iron latch of stout design.  Because of its lightness the unusual bracing adds considerably to its strength, and lessens the likelihood of its sagging. The wire brace from the left gate post to an adjoining post assures the added solidarity of the gate post itself.  The wire brace is of heavy gauge, and is tightened by inserting and rotating a stick between the two wires until all slack has been taken up.  The weight of wire is such that it will not unwind, and the hardwood stick or metal rod is then removed.  Should the gate or post sag at a later date the wire brace can be tightened further, as required.

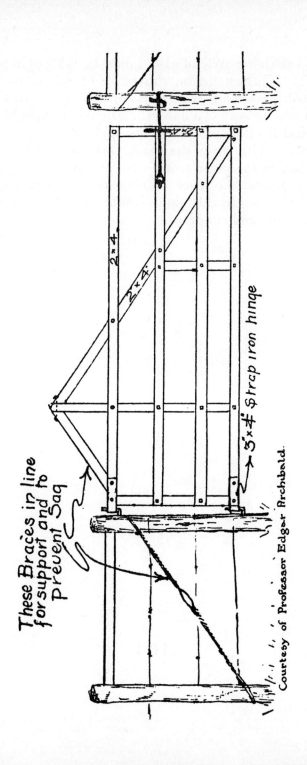

These Braces in line for support and to Prevent Sag

2ˣ4

2ˣ4

2ˣ4

3ˣ⅛ Strap iron hinge

Courtesy of Professor Edgar Archibald.

THIS sawhorse style of gate should be both light and strong. The fencing on either side of it is taken for granted. Its main feature is, of course, its lack of latch and hinges. To move the gate one merely lifted and slid it either way until one end was clear of the grooves. The main drawback then occurred when one had to carry the whole gate out of the way and lean it against the fence. Such a ten-foot board gate weighed considerable, and would be hard on the women folk and children.

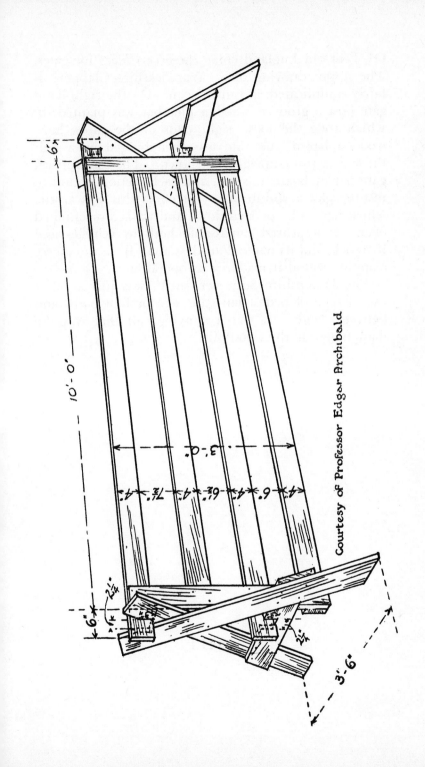

Courtesy of Professor Edgar Archbald

OUT of old England come these two ideas for gates. The upper drawing of a "Warwickshire Clapper" is fairly complicated, as can be seen. On the right-hand gate post a grooved wooden member was planted, in which rode the loose right ends of the gate. Each wooden bar of the gate was then hinged by a bolt through a stout upright, as shown. The left vertical gate bar or board was cut, and each section bound to insure against splintering. In effect this was a stile which had to be pressed down and walked or climbed over. It appeared impassable both to vehicles and livestock, and its name doubtless arose from the merry clapping sound it made in its operation.

The Hampshire Squeezer, or V, was just another useful type of pedestrian gateway, for foot paths and between fields. It was a straying calf that was the main nigger in the wood pile.

A Warwickshire "Clapper"

Courtesy of
Sir Charles Hagberg Wright,
London Library,
St. James's Square, London.

A Hampshire "V" or "Squeezer"

"I'M SITTING on the stile, Mary, where we sat side by side—"

The lower drawing wouldn't lend itself to courting too well, what with the separating pole barrier and the barbed wire. However it *is* a good example of an economical stile, taking but little room and being simple in construction.

Like the upper one, it was more comfortable for crossing with pails or other loads, such as someone in your arms.

# Front Step Stile

Made of 2 inch by 10 inch or 12 inch plank

Supplies easy approach and safe footing when carrying pails, etc.

# Side Step Stile

Simpler in construction and projects less into field than front step stile.

C.W.J.

THE wood fence stile herewith could scarcely be any more simple or primitive. Yet it appears sturdy and effective. The flat stone on the ground added a little to its appearance and made for solid rather than muddy footing in the wet English season. Strange, these customs of England, permitting common right of way.

What a fair, bonnie, timeless stone fence stile is the lower one. Look at the size of those boulders. One can just picture the moorland figure in the swinging plaid kilt making its way through the gloaming, with a skirl from the pipes echoing in the woodland and the glen.

## Wood Fence Stile

In use in many districts in England where ancient common right of way across private property exists.

## Stone Fence Stile

Typical of moorland and down country where wood is scarce.

C.W.J.

SUCH a beautiful and time-worn stile in the upper illustration. Everything about it bespeaks solidarity, and strength, and quiet timelessness. How odd and staunch are the metal straps banding over and bolted to the stout tree trunk which serves as the fence's upper member.

And what a very different feeling we get from the lower drawing. The graceful wooden turnstile within the lovely Tudor stone arched gateway leading to the formal gardens within. A pleasant note upon which to conclude our wanderings as fence viewers.

Courtesy of
Adam Strohm, Esq.
Detroit.

From "England Beautiful,"
by Wallace Nutting. ➔

# INDEX